WHAT ARE SAYING ABOUT
iBelong

iBelong is a masterpiece! For every believer seeking to have authentic relationships in their local church, for every leader desiring to connect with the hearts of the people they lead, and for families longing to share their lives in community, this book is a must-read! *iBelong* breaks down the walls of isolation and empowers believers with meaningful insight on how to not only fit, but flourish, in the house of God.—APOSTLE JANE HAMON, PASTOR, VISION CHURCH, SANTA ROSA BEACH, FL

With all the excuses removed and blessings established, there is no reason you should not be where you belong. Apostle Robert Gay provides powerful, practical ways to defeat the plans of the enemy and find your place of fulfillment and contribution—the place where you belong!—APOSTLE DEAN MITCHUM, DIRECTOR OF WORSHIP MINISTRIES FOR CHRISTIAN INTERNATIONAL, WORSHIP PASTOR, VISION CHURCH, SANTA ROSA BEACH, FL

Robert Gay's passion for building the church and leaders has always been strong and the tools God has revealed to him have helped me and thousands of readers who have entertained the present truth revelation in his books. He is a masterful author bringing deeper understanding to the reader, while giving tools that will help any minister or leader to build the Church. Robert's new book has a strong message for every leader to help understand the importance for every member of the local church and for the body of Christ to know the importance of belonging where God has planted them. Enjoy this book, and let it lead you to change while on your journey to successful leadership.—APOSTLE M. LEON WALTERS, PASTOR & APOSTLE, CHRISTIAN INTERNATIONAL FAMILY WORSHIP CENTER/CI CENTRAL, VERSAILLES, IN

In his 8th book, *iBelong*, acclaimed author, singer, and songwriter, Robert Gay, masterfully articulates the spiritual and practical importance of getting plugged-in and planted in a local church body. *iBelong* truly belongs in my library!—WILL OWEN, AUTHOR & PRESIDENT/CEO, JET BOAT PILOT, PANAMA CITY, FL

FINDING *YOUR* PLACE IN
THE *BODY OF CHRIST*

iBELONG

ROBERT GAY

Parsons Publishing House
Melbourne, Florida USA

iBelong—Finding Your Place in the Body of Christ
by Robert Gay

Parsons Publishing House
P. O. Box 410063
Melbourne, FL 32941
www.ParsonsPublishingHouse.com
Info@ParsonsPublishingHouse.com

Cover Art: Micah Gay

ISBN-13: 978-1-60273-111-0
ISBN-10: 1-60273-111-x
Library of Congress Control Number: 2019941894
Printed in the United States of America.
For World-Wide Distribution.

TABLE OF CONTENTS

FOREWORD by Bishop Bill Hamon   *vii*
PREFACE   *ix*
CHAPTER 1   iBelong   1
CHAPTER 2   iPartake   13
CHAPTER 3   iGather   27
CHAPTER 4   iFit   39
CHAPTER 5   iFunction   47
CHAPTER 6   iEngage   69
CHAPTER 7   iFlow   83
CHAPTER 8   iChange   97
CHAPTER 9   iGive   111
CHAPTER 10   iForgive   123
CHAPTER 11   iBelieve, Part 1   141
CHAPTER 12   iBelieve, Part 2   153
CHAPTER 13   iConnect   165
ABOUT THE AUTHOR   171

FOREWORD

by Bishop Bill Hamon

Bishop of Christian International Apostolic-Global Network

The revelation and wonderful truths presented by Robert Gay in this book come from years of preparation and learning to hear the voice of God and being inspired by the spirit of wisdom and revelation.

I have known Robert and Stacey for more than 30 years. Robert was our worship leader at CI Family Church and at our prophetic conferences for over 10 years. He became more than a worship leader. He became a prophetic songwriter expressing the truths of the Prophetic Movement.

In my book entitled ***Prophets and the Prophetic Movement***, I proclaimed Robert to be a prophetic minstrel to put music to the truths I was preaching, especially about Jesus being a Mighty Man of War and raising up a prophetic army. He was doing the same for me as Charles Wesley did for his brother, John Wesley, who was the founder of Methodism and pioneer of the Holiness Movement of the 1700s. Pages 119 through 121 (***Prophets and The Prophetic Movement***) mention a few of the hundreds of choruses Robert wrote and of the many CDs he recorded.

Robert has been and continues to be a man of God with integrity, wisdom, and a balanced presentation of truth.

Robert and I were traveling together overseas for ministry. While on the plane, Robert asked me what I thought about becoming a pastor of his own church. I bounced it off my spirit and said to Robert, "Yes, I believe it is God, and you will make a great pastor, and you will grow to 500 within a few years." Well, Robert has built a church and has exceeded over that 500 number. His church is one of the largest churches that I am Bishop of in the USA and some of the 3,000 churches I am Bishop of in the rest of the world.

There are two other books that Robert has written that I highly recommended to all our pastors, *Planted* and *Building Strong*. Now, *iBelong* is a masterpiece. Every Christian needs to read it, and every pastor should teach the truths and principles in this book to their congregation, but especially to their new members class.

Bless you, Robert, for blessing the Body of Christ with this very valuable book. You make me proud to be your Bishop and spiritual Papa to your family. Blessings to you and all who read this book.

Bill Hamon books include: *The Eternal Church, Prophets & Personal Prophecy; Prophets & the Prophetic Movement; Prophets, Pitfalls, & Principles; Apostles/Prophets & the Coming Moves of God; The Day of the Saints; Who Am I & Why Am I Here; Prophetic Scriptures Yet to be Fulfilled; 70 Reasons for Speaking in Tongues; How Can These Things Be?;* and *God's World War III.*

PREFACE

Some time ago, I received a call from a gentleman who had been part of our church body for about a decade. His family seemed to enjoy the ministry at the church tremendously. They were happy and joyous people and never complained about anything. Frankly, they were what most pastors consider model church members.

This family was highly complimentary of all the ministries within the church. During worship, they entered in and participated. They also listened attentively as the Word was taught and preached. It was apparent that they engaged in all aspects of the services. They were authentic and loving people.

As I continued my conversation with the gentleman on the phone, he stated they had been missing some services because they were visiting around to some other churches. Then he said this, "We just want to be where we fit." When he said that, I was taken back. For a moment I was speechless and didn't know what to say. I ended up replying to him, "Well, it's my desire for you to be where you fit."

I did not try to sway or convince him that they should remain at our church. Honestly, when people get to the point that they desire to go elsewhere, I have learned that appealing to them to stay produces very little fruit. I ended up wishing him and his family well. I expressed my appreciation for them and shared that if there was anything I could do for them in the future to call me.

The thing which surprised me the most in our conversation was the statement that they wanted to be where they fit. His comment insinuated that they didn't fit. From my superficial observation, they did fit. As far as I could tell they were receiving from the ministry. I didn't realize there was a problem. However, there was something within their heart that made them feel that they didn't fit.

After I thought about our conversation, I realized their feeling of failing to fit caused them to feel they didn't belong. Thus, the sense of belonging within them was not being fulfilled. My mind began to race to deduce why they believed they didn't fit. What was it that made them conclude they didn't belong anymore? After all, nothing had really changed since they started coming to the church a decade ago.

As I contemplated my conversation with him, there was one thing that stood out in my mind. That was this: there was presence with failure to function. They were in attendance, yet did nothing in the way of functioning within the church. There was no ministry group or fellowship group in which they were involved. Their only connection was attendance in the service and contributing in the offering. Other than that, there was no participation. They received, but failed to function. Since that time, we have initiated certain things in our church to help people get connected so they can feel and say, "iBelong!"

When people feel they don't fit or belong, it is typically because of their lack of connection and function within the local church. As a result, they fail to have a sense of investment or ownership and eventually fall by the way. I recognize that those who suffer from rejection will feel they don't belong regardless of what may be initiated to help them connect. However, pastors and leaders must make every attempt to help people connect and function within a church body.

Being a member of a church without functioning is like a plant without roots. It is the roots of a plant that cause it to remain stationary. A believer's function within the body of Christ is the root that keeps them in place. It is their function that causes them to possess a sense of belonging.

Jesus talked about those who had no root within themselves in the parable of the sower. I've concluded that some of the ones He was talking about were those who fail to function in the church. This can happen for a variety of reasons. However, roots are what keep you from being blown away.

There are many believers who are being blown away by the enemy because they fail to function. Consequentially, this makes them feel they don't fit, and they don't belong.

We must realize that this is the plan of the devil. He uses a believer's own failure to function within the church to take advantage of them. Remember this: it is the banana that gets separated from the bunch that gets peeled and eaten.

When people feel they don't belong, they separate. The enemy will do everything he can to prevent believers from getting connected and staying connected to a local church body. Why? It is because he has difficulty taking advantage of believers when they fit, function, and belong to a strong local church. He cannot peel and eat the banana that is connected to the bunch. There is divine protection afforded those who belong to a church body with a strong and loving pastor.

During the editing process of this writing, I had a dream. In the dream, I was walking on a concrete sidewalk that seemed to circle a large building. There were people that were walking on the sidewalk with me at various paces. I came upon some people that were walking slower than me, so I passed them on the right-hand side.

As I passed them I was praying in the Spirit (tongues). I heard the voice of one of the persons I passed praying in the Spirit also. I was happily surprised. I turned around to a young man that I distinguished was praying in that manner and shouted out, "We belong to the same tribe!" The moment I said that, he began to run and passed me. I started to chase after him while saying, "We belong to the same tribe!" He ran off and disappeared as I couldn't keep up with him.

The dream then shifted to where I was on the porch of this building that I had been walking around. There was an older gentleman with gray hair sitting in a chair around an outdoor table. He asked me for a writing pen. I looked around and saw pens, but they belonged to other people. I continued searching until I found one that didn't belong to someone else. Interesting enough, these were all pens with our church name (High Praise) on them. I gave the pen to him, and he began writing. The dream ended.

After I awakened, I began to think about this dream and asked the Holy Spirit the meaning. I immediately had illumination and revelation.

The sidewalk in the dream represents our walk with God—our purpose and destiny. The building represents the Church and how it is to be built through every member functioning. The young man represents those with unrealized potential in the kingdom of God. I represent leadership within the church who has the responsibility to identify and release the potential of others. The older gray-haired gentleman on the porch represents wisdom. I believe that me giving the older gentleman the pen is now the writing of this book and the ability for wisdom to be articulated.

When I passed the young man and turned to him and said, "We belong to the same tribe," there was an immediate acceleration in the young man's pace. I believe this speaks of the empowerment that happens when we understand that we belong, fit, and are accepted. When this young man heard that we belonged to the same tribe, he began to run at a much faster pace. He was energized and strengthened to move faster when the sense of belonging was released within his life.

I believe the same thing that happened to the young man in my dream will happen to you as you read this book. I believe that you will be empowered in your walk with God. I believe that you will run faster and do more than previous generations. I believe there will be a sense of belonging that will arise within your heart so you can run the race with patience and persistence.

This book is written to help members of the Church fit, function, and belong. This is the plan of God for every believer. His desire is for none of us to be the "Lone Ranger." God wants us to be plugged in and connected. My desire is that after reading this book, you will be able to know and say, "iBelong!"

CHAPTER 1

iBelong

> **BELONGING IS SOMETHING THAT WE ARE PROGRAMMED TO EXPERIENCE BY OUR CREATOR. MAN IS DEFICIENT WHEN HE BELONGS TO NOTHING.**

"And the LORD God said, 'It is not good that man should be alone; I will make him a helper comparable to him'" (Genesis 2:18).

I believe within the heart of every human being resides a desire to belong. At the time of creation, God said, "It is not good for man to be alone." A divine principle was established that man was not to be by himself. He needed a helper. So, God created woman.

In creating Eve and placing her with Adam, God established the foundation for the family. This was to be the foundation of all societal structures. The man and woman were to come together to procreate and expand their family. Thus, the first sense of belonging that all humans desire and are to experience is that of family.

1

As families expanded, communities would arise and develop. The first communities were those who had a common family connection. In ancient Israel, there were twelve tribes. Those who belonged to a particular tribe possessed a shared family connection. This was not something they chose. It was chosen for them based upon their family connection and belonging.

Families who united together became a community. Some benefits were afforded to individuals who were connected and joined to the communities that developed. There was protection, safety, and mutual assistance derived by all those involved. The principle of divine synergism was activated and enacted because of the combined efforts of unified individuals and families.

Belonging is Good

In our society today, we can see this principle in action on numerous levels. The principle of belonging is enacted far beyond family connections. We see it displayed throughout our culture. It is exhibited in schools, clubs, social media, politics, etc. Even more so, we see it demonstrated in the church.

This is not an evil thing; it is good. Remember: God said that it was "not good" for man to be alone and by himself with no sense of belonging. Therefore, it is good when man is working alongside others with a common goal and purpose.

I remember when I was in school, there were various organizations and clubs in which you could participate.

Typically, your involvement would be based upon your interest. I was involved in the band because I played the trumpet. My perceived connection with the school was that I was a band member. I recognize that the primary purpose of school is academic in nature; however, most students are not going to feel a sense of belonging based solely on their educational classes.

My sense of belonging to the school stemmed from me belonging to the band; it was my place of function within the school. The band program was a place I could express my interest and gifting. It was a point of connection for me. It caused me to feel some sense of ownership and responsibility within the school. I was not merely coming to learn; I was coming to contribute.

Giver and Not a Taker

As a part of the band, I would stay after school for up to two hours a day during football season when we would practice for half-time shows. It was the sense of belonging that caused the band members to do this. While everyone else got away from the campus as quickly as possible after the dismissal bell rang, we would stay to practice and rehearse our performances. We were not paid to do so; rather, it was a sense of belonging that dictated it.

The sense of belonging will cause you to be a giver and not a taker. It will cause you to participate and function as a part of something larger than yourself. You will find delight in being a blessing to someone else.

Two are better than one, Because they have a good reward for their labor. For if they fall, one will lift up his companion. But woe to him who is alone when he falls, For he has no one to help him up. Again, if two lie down together, they will keep warm; But how can one be warm alone? Though one may be overpowered by another, two can withstand him. And a threefold cord is not quickly broken (Ecclesiastes 4:9-12).

We see in the above Scripture that there is help, strength, protection, and safety when individuals are not alone. The Bible goes so far as to say, "Woe, to him who is alone." "Woe" is a word that we use today to mean "STOP!" I believe the Lord is saying that those who want to go it alone should STOP. They should reconsider their ways and understand that God has great things prepared for them as they connect with others in the body of Christ. There is so much more God can and will do through us when we choose to belong.

Programmed to Belong by the Creator

Belonging is something that we are programmed to experience by our Creator. When God created man, He programmed him with the need to belong. Man is deficient when he belongs to nothing. This need to belong is embedded in our makeup.

A child who does not belong to a family is considered orphaned. Numerous psychological and sociological issues have been linked to children deserted by their parents.

This is not the fault of the child, but it still creates many problems within their lives. Why is this? It is because there is a need that is deep-seated within man that can only be satisfied by experiencing a sense of belonging.

When people fail to realize there are divine mechanisms that fulfill this need to belong, they attempt to reach out to find fulfillment through fleshly and sinful means. These improper fleshly manifestations have resulted in the creation of gangs and other illicit organizations which provide an illegitimate fulfillment of the legitimate need to belong. These kinds of groups are the counterfeit that the devil, our adversary, desires for people. It is the substitute for the real and authentic that God created.

Belonging to the Family of God

God first created man to need a relationship with Him. In other words, we need to belong to the family of God. It is through the blood of Jesus that we can now be a part of that family. Through believing on the name of the Lord and receiving the atoning work accomplished through His death, burial, and resurrection, we are adopted as sons and daughters of the Almighty God. This is the first and most important entity to which we are to belong, the family of God.

As a part of the family of God, we are given an identity that supersedes all others. That identity is that we are children of God, and we belong to Him. It takes precedent because it is the priority; it is the highest of all identities. It trumps any other fleshly or natural identity. This identity establishes to whom we belong. We belong

5

to Jesus; we no longer belong to sin or the devil. We are a part of the family of God. Hallelujah!

When Adam was created, God would commune with him in the cool of the evening; He would walk and talk with Adam. God was reinforcing that Adam belonged to Him. God was stating that Adam's place of belonging was at His side. Man did not belong anywhere else but in a place of communion with the Father.

When Adam and Eve sinned, they lost that place of belonging. They were no longer able to commune with the Father in the cool of the evening. They were evicted from their home in the Garden of Eden—two lost souls with no place of belonging.

I Love It When a Plan Comes Together

After the fall of man, a plan was enacted to regain what man had lost. Primarily, he had lost his place of belonging. Although man was programmed to be close and intimate with the Father God, sin became the roadblock. Sin became the wall that could not be traversed over or around which separated man from the place where he belonged.

In the fullness of time, the Father God sent His Son, Jesus, to the earth. He came to take the sin of all humanity. He came to pay the price that was required for man's sin to be blotted out and removed. In doing so, man could now find his place of belonging once again. Jesus paid the price so that all who believed on Him could once again belong to the Father God just like Adam did in the beginning.

As Christians, the first sense of belonging we should possess is that we belong to Father God. We are a part of the kingdom of God. We have been translated out of the kingdom of darkness and into the kingdom of light. We were once lost, but now we are found. God's grace has brought us to the place where we belong. This is the most important understanding that anyone can possess: we belong to Jesus.

Belonging to the Body of Christ

However, everything doesn't stop with belonging to the Lord. We must equally understand that since we belong to Jesus, we also belong to the body of Christ. We are a part of His body, the Church.

> "Now you are the body of Christ, and members individually" (1 Corinthians 12:27).

Since we belong to Jesus, we belong to His body. Belonging to the Lord means we equally belong to the body of Christ. Why is this? It is because you cannot separate Jesus and His body. They are inseparable and function together; they cannot function independently of each other.

Just like your head needs your body, so Jesus needs His body. He cannot thrive and function without His body. Likewise, we cannot live, survive, or thrive without the head. The head belongs to the body, and the body belongs to the head.

Belonging to the Church

Every individual member of the body of Christ needs a place of belonging where their ministry and spiritual gifts can be expressed. That place of belonging for the members of the body of Christ is the local church. The local church is the physical manifestation on earth of the spiritual body of Christ. It is the headquarters that God has established for the body of Christ to function and move in locales around the globe. It is the base from which the body of Christ is enabled to minister and reach the world.

Every believer needs to belong to a local church. The need and desire to belong will not be totally fulfilled without belonging to a local church body. The reason for this is that belonging is not manifested through merely an acknowledgment of being saved. Belonging is expressed and fulfilled through the expression of one's gifting and ability. These expressions of one's gifts are housed and empowered within the functioning of a local church body.

Belonging Enables Expression

When I was in school and a member of the band, I was given the opportunity for musical expression by playing the trumpet. Regardless of how well someone may have played the horn, if they did not belong to the band, they could not play there. The opportunity was not afforded based merely on one's ability, but rather their connection to the organization. This meant they attended classes, extra practices, and rehearsals. Likewise, when someone belongs to a local church, the place of connection creates the opportunity for expression.

Many believers could avoid needless frustration if they would only choose to belong to a local church. They would have others there to help them in different seasons of their lives. Protection and safety would be afforded them through God-ordained covering and accountability. They would no longer feel like the lone sheep wandering in the wilderness. They would have an assurance that they belong to something that will bring great benefit to them and their families.

Many people receive Jesus as their Savior, yet continue to live without a sense of belonging. This could be avoided if these new believers would immediately connect themselves to a local church. They would find a place that embraces them along with other Christians to help them grow as new believers. They would then be able to say, "iBelong."

"To the praise of the glory of His grace, by which He made us accepted in the Beloved" (Ephesians 1:6).

Going back to Adam, the moment he sinned, he was separated from God. He made coverings out of fig leaves to hide himself; he felt as if he no longer belonged in the presence of the Lord. The shame that sin produced had separated him from the place that he belonged. He was ultimately banned from the Garden of Eden and lost his place of belonging. Adam experienced rejection as a result of sin.

God enacted a plan whereby man could regain acceptance and the sense of belonging. Jesus came and paid the price for our sin and made a way for us to have relationship with the Father. Through the grace of God, we are now accepted; we now have a place to belong. The place of belonging has been restored to us. We are now accepted by the Father, and we belong!

Acceptance Trumps Rejection

In the early days of my ministry (early 1980s), I would unknowingly minister at times from a place of rejection. My pastor recognized this and prayed for me. I was delivered from that spirit of rejection. That spirit caused me to lash out when people did not respond correctly. I was not doing it consciously or deliberately; however, I was reacting from a place of hurt and rejection.

We must understand that when people experience rejection or feel rejected, they will then reject others. Therefore, a vicious circle is created. That circle is: you reject me, and I reject you; therefore, I don't belong. We start to live as misfits because we feel rejected or have a spirit of rejection operating within our lives.

The greatest tool that we possess to combat the spirit of rejection is the Word of God. It declares that we are accepted in the beloved. In other words, "iBelong." I belong to Jesus. I belong to the body of Christ. I belong to the church. If you feel rejected or isolated, begin to declare, "I am accepted, and iBelong."

The Church—A Place of Belonging

God has ordained that the church be a place of belonging. The local church should not be a dead, dry place where services are regularly conducted, and people assemble out of religious obligation. Neither should it be a place where people convene to sit for an hour or two and receive ministry, yet never contribute. God has designed the local church to be a life-giving place where believers gather for mutual edification as every member supplies their divine purpose. It is meant to be a place where everyone can say, "iBelong."

While there are many things on the earth to which we may never have the opportunity to belong, we can make a choice to belong to a local church body. No one votes as to whether you can belong to a church (at least not in our church). It is a choice that is made by the one who desires to belong. It begins with the choice of making Jesus the Lord of your life. At that moment, you become part of the Church (all those who are born again) and position yourself to belong to a local church. I tell everyone in our local church, "If you are good enough for Jesus, then you're good enough for me."

The Church—A Living Organism

Belonging to a local church begins with your commitment to Jesus. The church is not a club that you join. Rather, it is a living organism. That's the reason Paul refers to it as the "body of Christ." Since Jesus is alive, so is His body. Therefore, the local church is to be the living expression of Jesus and His ongoing ministry within the earth.

11

The moment that you become a Christian, you belong to the universal, multi-member body of Christ. This means that you belong to a family that is comprised of all who have surrendered their lives to Jesus—those who have made Him Lord. The next step after accepting Jesus as Savior is to get connected to a local church body. We must all find that place to belong.

There is a place that God has ordained for us to belong. That place is within a local church body which is moving forward in truth, understanding, and pursuit of the purpose of God. I have found that the Holy Spirit will be faithful to show us that place if we are willing to listen to Him. He will reveal to us the place that God has called us to belong. As we connect ourselves, there will be blessings reaped within our lives. We will move beyond the frustration of being alone, separated, and disconnected. Instead, we will receive a sense of belonging. We will be empowered to boldly say, "iBelong."

CHAPTER 2

iPartake

"THE DIVINE NATURE IS GREATER THAN ANY OTHER NATURAL IDENTIFIER."

As His divine power has given to us all things that pertain to life and godliness, through the knowledge of Him who called us by glory and virtue, by which have been given to us exceedingly great and precious promises, that through these you may be partakers of the divine nature, having escaped the corruption that is in the world through lust (2 Peter 1:3-4).

Many believers do not realize the fullness of everything that they received at the moment of their salvation. The Bible tells us that we become new creatures in Christ Jesus (2 Corinthians 5:17). It literally means something was created that never existed before. We see in the above Scripture that we are made partakers of God's divine nature. Numerous other things take place the moment that we are born-again. There is a total transformation of the inner man as one receives the gift of eternal life.

13

Embracing and Understanding the Divine Nature

Becoming a Christian and being saved is more than acquiring a fire insurance policy that keeps you from the lake of fire. It is more than merely a ticket to heaven on the good "Old Gospel Ship." It means that you have passed from death into life. It means that the old man is dead. It means that the grace of God has been received, and now there is power to live victorious over sin.

To hear some Christians talk, you would think that salvation was merely something they received to prevent them from experiencing the punishment of hell. They fail to see salvation as a supernatural event that empowered them. Rather, they see salvation as the great escape. The full understanding of the divine nature has not been comprehended within their lives. They became partakers of the divine nature the moment they said "yes" to Jesus; however, they fail to realize the fullness of what they received.

To be an effective member of the body of Christ and function properly within the local church, it is imperative that believers embrace the spiritual revelation of partaking of the divine nature. Without this understanding, believers will not grow in the manner God intends. Neither will they function fully in the manner they should operate within the church.

Those who fail to embrace the understanding of the divine nature will live defeated lifestyles. Their profession will be that they are merely sinners saved by grace. They will say that they are only human and are just prone to fail. We must understand that the eternal life that we have received is so much greater. It is designed to cause us to live in victory and triumph while we are on this earth.

The Word of God says we are "partakers" of His nature. The word "partaker" means a sharer or associate. The Greek root word means to be held in common or shared by all. Peter is pointing out that once someone is saved, there is a common nature that is shared by all members of the body of Christ. We are interconnected with one another because we are all partakers of that same divine nature. It is the very DNA of Father God; you and I possess the same spiritual DNA of Jesus!

New Nature Means New Identity

The nature of God that I received at the time of salvation is the same nature that Christians in China receive at the time of salvation. We all share something in common. The divine nature that we all receive is greater than natural identification, national heritage, ethnic identity, or political persuasion. It supersedes all other distinct unique characteristics that would otherwise make us different. The blood of Jesus enables all who believe to partake of the same nature regardless of family background, skin pigmentation, or financial status. The divine nature is greater than any other natural identifier.

God has designed His nature (the new nature) to be our primary identification. It is the new man (new creation) that is made in the image of Christ. The new man that you have been made in Christ is greater than who you are in the natural arenas of life. It does not cancel out or negate your career, natural family, gender, national heritage, or racial distinctiveness, etc. However, it supersedes them all! Praise God!

This is so important to understand because these natural things are what the devil will attempt to use to divide the body of Christ. The enemy will endeavor to emphasize our different backgrounds, political leanings, national heritage, ethnicity, educational background, or financial status to create a point of contention. **We must resist the ploy of the enemy by focusing on the fact that we all share God's divine nature.** This is that of which we have all been made partakers; it is our point of commonality. The divine nature is what makes us all belong to the same body—the body of Christ.

Eternal Life Now

> And this is the testimony: that God has given us eternal life, and this life is in His Son. He who has the Son has life; he who does not have the Son of God does not have life (1 John 5:11-12).

One of the first understandings that we should possess concerning the divine nature is that eternal life begins the moment that we are saved. Eternal life is the very nature of God. Jesus said that He came so that man could have life and that more abundantly. The nature of God is a life-giving nature. When God created Adam and formed him from the dust of the earth, He breathed the breath of life into him. He did not leave Adam a lifeless corpse; He gave Adam life which demonstrates God's nature.

Likewise, the divine nature of which we have been made partakers gives life. The divine nature is God's life-giving, life-producing, and life-propagating nature that is designed to affect every area of a Christian's being. It is intended to affect our spirit, soul, and body. It is purposed to produce in your home, church, and place of employment. It is not limited to any place, time, space, or moment. The switch was turned on the moment you were saved, and it can only be turned off by you. So, don't turn it off, keep it on! Allow His divine nature to be manifested in and through you.

Many have thought that eternal life is something that begins when you physically die. However, eternal life has nothing to do with the existence of your physical body. Eternal life began the moment your old man died. It began the moment you were born-again. The very life of God was imparted to your spirit man. The real you, your spirit man, was resurrected as you received the gift of eternal life. Eternal life is now! We are not waiting until our body dies; eternal life has already started.

The phrase "eternal life" is comprised of two Greek words. The word "eternal" means perpetual and never-ending; the word "life" comes from the Greek word *zoe* which literally means to live and possess vitality.

So, the fact that eternal life is perpetual and never-ending means that it never ceases. It is continual in its purpose and productivity. It can't be turned off unless we do it ourselves. However, why would anyone ever want to turn eternal life off?

Living vs. Existing

The very life that was in Jesus is now living within us. We have been made partakers of His divine nature—the nature of eternal life. Just as the life in Jesus has no end, neither does the life in you; it is eternal. His life is intended to cause you to do more than merely have a natural existence on earth.

When I was growing up, there were times that we observed those who were greatly blessed in natural things. We would say, "Wow, they are really living." We never said that about anyone who was on Skid Row; we didn't say that about anyone who was sick and dying. It was always said concerning those who exhibited a manifested blessing.

There are many believers today who are merely existing when the Father wants them to live. His eternal life that they received at the time of salvation was never designed to be hidden from manifestation. It was designed to be released within every dimension of their being.

Eternal life is to be in existence in our home, family, career, health, and finances. The life of God will move beyond our spirit man if we allow it to disseminate into the other areas of our lives. Allow His life to flow through every arena of your life. Say "yes" to eternal life!

The New Creation

"Therefore, if anyone is in Christ, he is a new creation; old things have passed away; behold, all things have become new" (2 Corinthians 5:17).

When someone is born-again, they become a new creation. The Greek word translated "creation" was originally coined by Jewish rabbis which was used to describe someone who had converted from idolatry to Judaism. It indicated a change that had transpired in the life of an individual. No longer would they follow idols; they would now follow Jehovah God.

The apostle Paul then uses the phrase "new creation" when describing the transformation within the life of one who believes on Jesus. This word "new" means unprecedented, uncommon, and unheard. That means the moment you partake of the divine nature, you become an unprecedented individual, an uncommon human being, and unheard of in supernatural ability! Can somebody SHOUT?

My Old Man is Dead

Paul goes on to say that old things have passed away. When someone dies, we say they passed away. So, the old things are dead; all of it was crucified with Christ and buried with Him. The old things are the old man and sin nature, along with his beliefs and behaviors. Those things have passed away; it means they no longer exist. The old man fashioned after sin no longer exists. Your old man died the day you received Jesus.

It is vital for believers to identify with the new man in Christ rather than the old man who is dead. It is imperative that we begin to see ourselves through the eyes of the new man rather than the retrospect of the old. You will impair yourself spiritually if you continue to identify with your old man. Why should you think about the old man you were that is now dead when you can think about the new man you are who is alive in Christ Jesus? Think about it.

Begin to declare daily that you are a new creation in Christ Jesus. Reinforce this truth within your life through the confession of your mouth. Rehearse your salvation experience when you passed from death into life.

We have looked at Romans 10:10 which declares, "With the mouth confession is made unto salvation," as a principle that applies only to the moment we are saved. However, this is a principle that is perpetual within the life of a believer. The more you confess and identify with the new man, the more it will take preeminence within your life.

The Righteousness of God

"For He made Him who knew no sin to be sin for us, that we might become the righteousness of God in Him" (2 Corinthians 5:21).

The fact that we are now righteous is because we have been partakers of the divine nature. Since Jesus is righteous, we are righteous. His righteousness has now been imparted to us because we now possess His nature.

Righteousness means right standing with God. We have right standing with God as if we had never sinned or done anything wrong. The blood of Jesus has cleansed us, and through the power of His resurrection, we have been justified by faith. We can now boldly come before the throne of grace because we are righteous.

The consciousness of sin will cause one to be timid before God. The consciousness of righteousness will cause one to walk in authority boldly. We are exhorted to come boldly before the throne of grace (Hebrews 4:16). The only way this can take place is through the full realization of our righteousness through Jesus Christ.

We are not those who attempt to sneak in the back door of heaven hoping that we can snatch a blessing before anyone realizes it. Instead, we come boldly announcing our arrival and receive the promise that Jesus already made available to us. Our approach to the throne of God is bold and fearless when we understand righteousness. Timidity and apprehension exit your life when you realize you are righteous.

I am not righteous because of what I have done, but rather because I am a partaker of His nature. His nature is righteousness. There is no sin in His nature; therefore, there is no sin in my nature. Within my flesh, as Paul said, dwells no good thing (Romans 7:18). However, my flesh is not my nature. My nature—the divine nature—is sinless and righteous.

The Process of Sanctification

The ongoing process within the life of a believer is to get what is on the inside to be in manifestation on the outside. This process is referred to as sanctification. While we are already sanctified through the blood of Jesus, there is the continual sanctifying work of the Holy Spirit that is ongoing within our lives. You are to put on the new man that is created in the image of God; you are to clothe yourself with the new man in Christ. Let the real you be what you manifest.

I've heard some believers say in moments when they allowed their flesh to dictate their behavior, "Well, that's just me." However, that was not them at all. Their behavior was not revealing the divine nature at that moment. Their conduct was not exhibiting God's righteousness.

As believers, we must realize the importance of renewing our minds to what the Bible says concerning who we are, what we have, what we can do, and how we should live in Christ. We must also receive and appropriate healing and deliverance in all areas of our lives where the enemy previously possessed a right to render his rule. As we allow the Holy Spirit to reveal these things to us and we receive the fullness of His deliverance and healing, we will begin to live our lives differently. We will live as the righteousness of God in Christ, and it will be demonstrated throughout our lives.

Heirs of God

> For as many as are led by the Spirit of God, these are sons of God. For you did not receive the spirit of bondage again to fear, but you received the Spirit of adoption by whom we cry out, "Abba, Father." The Spirit Himself bears witness with our spirit that we are children of God, and if children, then heirs—heirs of God and joint heirs with Christ, if indeed we suffer with Him, that we may also be glorified together (Romans 8:14-17).

The realization that you are a child of God will shape your disposition toward the Father and the family of God. The understanding that you are an heir of God will release within you the ability to receive all that He desires for you.

There is a reason that Jesus was referred to as "The Son," and now we are called sons. We should see ourselves as sons (regardless of our gender) just like Jesus is the Son. Jesus is not only Lord of our lives, but He is also our elder brother. He is the first-born among many brethren (Romans 8:29). While He is the first Son, we are also sons. The Father sees us just like He sees Jesus. Praise God!

That's the reason we are joint-heirs (equal-heirs). You cannot be an equal-heir if you are not on an equal plane. If you are less than the Son, Jesus, then you cannot be a joint-heir. Think about it!

My Father's House

On most Sunday afternoons after our church services end, my family and I go to my parents' house. My father and mother owned a catering business for many years, and they feel that part of their ministry is to prepare a meal for our family who are all ministering on Sunday mornings.

When I come to my father's house, I don't ask permission to enter the house. I open the door and enter. I don't ask if I can get something to drink; I know where my father keeps all of his beverages. I go to the refrigerator where he keeps them, and I take one. I will even begin to munch on some of the things that are on the counter waiting to be served.

If anyone else in the neighborhood were to do such a thing, it would raise some eyebrows. If anyone else who is not a member of the family began to conduct themselves in such a manner, something would be said. However, I'm not merely anyone else. I'm not a neighborhood acquaintance. I AM A SON; I AM AN HEIR.

Too many believers are living in the Kingdom like neighborhood acquaintances rather than sons and heirs. They live below the privilege that has been afforded them. It's time to recognize who you are in Christ. You are a son of the God Almighty and a joint-heir with Christ Jesus. Live like it!

It is because I am a son of God that I know iBelong. It is because I am an equal heir with Christ that I know iBelong. It is because I am righteous that I know iBelong. It is because I am a new creation that I know iBelong. It is because of His blood that I know iBelong. It is because iPartake that I know iBelong.

CHAPTER 3

iGather

WHEN WE LOVE GOD, WE WILL LOVE THE CHURCH THAT JESUS PURCHASED WITH HIS BLOOD.

> And let us consider one another in order to stir up love and good works, not forsaking the assembling of ourselves together, as is the manner of some, but exhorting one another, and so much the more as you see the Day approaching (Hebrews 10:24-25).

One time a person came to me and said, "I don't need to go to church to be a Christian." At the time, I didn't reply to this individual because I could tell they were wanting to argue and debate. I think every believer recognizes that going to church doesn't make you a Christian any more than working in a garage makes you an automobile. A man and a woman living together doesn't make them married. However, married people should live together (and unmarried people shouldn't). Christians should go to church!

In the above passage of Scripture, we see that the assembling of believers is a command. It is not merely a suggestion or recommendation. Gathering together with those of like precious faith is not an option in the life of a Christian. It is a necessary component that will aid in the spiritual growth and function of all believers. Every Christian should be able to say "iGather."

The unfortunate statistic is that only a small percentage (less than half) of all Christians in the United States regularly attend church at least once a week. The national average for believers is they attend a church service approximately once every two to three weeks. This is dreadful! The average church attendance is far less than what it was decades ago despite a greater number of churches which are more conveniently located. I believe this needs to be corrected. The first thing we must do is make church attendance a priority in our lives. Yes, it should be a priority!

The majority of Christians are faithful to their place of employment. They have disciplined themselves to get up and go to work daily, even if they don't feel like it (which is a good thing). Yet, when it comes to church attendance, they go when it is convenient. If it is going to require any effort for them to show up, they stay home. What does this say about our dedication to the Lord? What does this say about our commitment to the body of Christ? We need to closely examine our priorities and place God back at the top.

Loving God Means Loving His People

When we love God, we will also love the people of God. When we love God, we will love the church that Jesus purchased with His blood. The reality is that we cannot say that we love God and despise the church. According to the apostle John, to do so is to speak and live a lie (1 John 4:20). John said that if we cannot love our brother (the church) whom we have seen, how can we love God whom we have not seen?

When we truly love someone, we desire to spend time with them. We want to be around them. We make plans to be with them on a regular basis. Why? It is because we love them.

When my wife and I were dating (before we were married), we would talk on the phone every moment we were able. I would go over to her house and sit with her and her parents. We would visit together and converse or watch something on television. I would regularly take her to dinner where we would sit and talk for hours. We spent time together.

We did this because we were in love with each other. We desired to be together. I wanted to "gather" with her. Likewise, when we are in love with Jesus and His church (His body), we will desire to gather with those of like precious faith. There will be something within us that compels us to be with other members of the body of Christ.

The plan of God is that iBelong to a local church body. Therefore, iGather! We are exhorted to gather on a regular basis because it is essential.

Gathering together is one of the primary things that we do when belonging to any organization. If you belong to a social club or organization, there are times designated for the gathering of those who belong. If your children are involved in sports activities, there are both practices and games that they are required to attend. If iBelong to the team, then iGather with the team. I will attend the practices and games.

The same principle applies to believers and the local church. To belong to a local church means that you attend the services regularly. Belonging implies involvement. Belonging means that iGather with those that comprise the local church body where God has called me to be planted.

Planted in the House

Those who are planted in the house of the LORD Shall flourish in the courts of our God. They shall still bear fruit in old age; They shall be fresh and flourishing (Psalm 92:13-14).

In this passage of Scripture, we see a promise to those who are planted in the house of the Lord—the local church. The Psalmist declares that they will flourish in the courts of the Lord. The word "flourish" means to bud and blossom. Fruitfulness is the by-product of gathering together in the name of the Lord. There is opportunity for one to spiritually flourish as they allow themselves to be planted in a local church.

When we are planted in the house, we will flourish in the courts. The courts represent the things that you do outside the house. God's promise is there will be blessing released within your life outside the church as you are faithful to be planted in the church. You will flourish in the areas of education, career, employment, family, etc.

One of the first things involved in being planted is gathering together. You cannot be planted within the house if you never go to the house. There may be some extenuating circumstances that prevent some people from regular attendance. However, this is not the norm. Most people who fail to gather together do so because of choices they make. The reality is that failure to gather together regularly only hurts the ones who fail to gather. They are the ones who are negatively affected. Unfortunately, they forfeit many promises and blessings that God has planned for them.

God promises blessing and prosperity to those who are planted in His house—the local church. This means blessing will flow into the lives of those who gather together regularly. They will receive greater measures of God's blessing than those who fail to gather.

All Things Work Together

Regular church attendance alone is not a magic formula that will cure everything in your life. It is not the one and only thing that you do as a Christian that will cause your life to be changed and blessed. However, going to church regularly is a great place to get the ball rolling.

Faith will arise as you receive the Word. It is because faith comes by hearing the Word preached. This will, in turn, make way for you to receive healing, deliverance, and breakthrough. Being in an atmosphere where the Spirit of the Lord is moving and ministering will cause spiritual transformation and change. Gathering with other believers will cause you to be strengthened and encouraged. Obedience to God's command to gather together will enact the blessings of obedience within your life (Deuteronomy 28). These blessings affect your spirit, soul, and body. This is afforded to those who regularly gather together.

The things that are derived from gathering will work together to produce good fruit within your life. Paul said, "We know all things work together for good to those who love God" (Romans 8:28). Could it be that the ones who "love God" are those who love the church also? Could it be that those who "love God" are those who regularly gather together? Could it be that those who can rightfully say that all things are working together for their good are those who can also say "iGather?" My answer to all these questions is "Yes!"

Many believers quote Romans 8:28 when they are faced with adversity. However, they fail to have a correct understanding of the verse and thus create an incorrect application. When Paul said, "All things work together for good," he was not stating that everything that happens within your life is there to work for your good. A contextual study will reveal he was stating that as we love God, pursue our divine purpose, then cooperate and co-labor with the work of the Holy Spirit, all these things will work for our good.

When you gather, you are cooperating with the work of the Holy Spirit. You are a doer of the Word. You are working the Word through your obedience. It is then that you can say, "All these things are working together for my good!"

Here is a testimony that was given by a member of our local church body.

> *I could count on one hand the times I had been in a church as a youth. I was born-again at nineteen. Two years later in fear and trepidation, I finally committed to obeying God's command not to forsake the assembling of yourselves together. I didn't know anyone at this church and didn't know what to expect, **but it was there that I found a place to belong**. I found brothers and sisters that I had more in common with than my earthly family. We had the same goals; we spoke the same language; we cared about the same things.*
>
> *The Bible says, "God sets the solitary in families" (Psalm 68:6, NKJV). In my church family, I found a group of people who were working toward a common goal to promote and expand the kingdom of God. I found my eternal purpose while being planted in a local church.*

It's also through faithful membership in a church where iron will sharpen iron. Day by day and service by service, I have had the rough edges worn off of my personality, motivation, character, and morals. I was not just there for the good times to have my ears tickled; when I became planted, I heard the whole counsel of God taught.

I found that when I became firmly rooted in a local body, I began the journey of being molded and shaped into the image of Jesus. I'm grateful to be a work in progress for His glory.

In the first part of this testimony, you will notice that as they gathered, they found a place to belong. Gathering is a part of belonging. Gathering together promotes a sense of belonging. You can never belong until you first gather and meet. Those who fail to gather will ultimately feel isolated, as though they don't belong. This is the trap of the enemy.

Separation—Satan's Strategy

"Be sober, be vigilant; because your adversary the devil walks about like a roaring lion, seeking whom he may devour" (1 Peter 5:8).

Many years ago, I heard Bishop Bill Hamon say this, "It is the banana that gets separated from the bunch that gets peeled and eaten." I quoted it earlier in this book. That phrase stuck with me. Although it can seem a little comical, there is tremendous truth held in that statement.

34

There is nothing more that the devil wants to do than peel you and devour you. Peter said that the devil is our enemy, and he is looking for those he can eat. The devil is looking for his next meal. Notice that Peter said the devil seeks out someone that he MAY devour. That means he can't devour everyone. One of the things that will provide protection for you is gathering with other believers in the house of the Lord.

The Psalmist David spoke of this kingdom principle:

> One thing I have desired of the LORD, That will I seek: That I may dwell in the house of the LORD All the days of my life, To behold the beauty of the LORD, And to inquire in His temple. For in the time of trouble He shall hide me in His pavilion; In the secret place of His tabernacle He shall hide me; He shall set me high upon a rock (Psalm 27:4-5).

David said that in the time of trouble God would hide us in His pavilion. He is saying that we can find refuge and strength as we gather with those of like precious faith. There is love, care, comfort, and grace that can be ministered. There is healing and deliverance that we can receive. There is divine protection that can be found within the place of covering where God has called us to gather and participate.

James said that we are to confess our faults one to another and pray for one another that we may be healed (James 5:16). This cannot be done in our homes by ourselves.

This is done in face-to-face gatherings with other members of the body of Christ. It's done in the local church gathering. Healing flows when we gather.

Jesus Gathered Faithfully

At the beginning of this chapter, we read Hebrews 10:25 which declares explicitly that believers are not to forsake assembling together. The Greek word that is translated "assembling" is *episunagoge*. It is where we get the English word "synagogue." The synagogue was a regular gathering place for the people of God.

> So He came to Nazareth, where He had been brought up. And as His custom was, He went into the synagogue on the Sabbath day, and stood up to read (Luke 4:16).

It was in the synagogue that Jesus took the Book of Isaiah and read. It is interesting to note that Jesus did not sporadically go to the synagogue. It was his normal behavior. Jesus was a regular attendee. Yes, Jesus went to church. He was faithful. Jesus could say, "iGather."

Notice that Luke points out that it was Jesus' custom to go to the synagogue. This means that it was His habit; He did it every Sabbath. He was not a twice a month attendee; He was faithful in His attendance. He was not a spiritual floater. Jesus was planted, and He gathered together with others. He was not a spiritual hermit in hibernation.

What is interesting about Jesus' faithfulness to the synagogue is that He was not in agreement with the teachers of the law. He would later refer to them as hypocrites, snakes, and whitewashed tombs. Regardless, Jesus still had a commitment to be in the house of the Lord.

I understand there may be a season where believers might have difficulty locating exactly where God wants them. I also understand there are some places that may not fit your spiritual taste. However, if Jesus could go to the synagogue and tolerate the teachers of the Law and their powerless preaching, you can certainly overlook some of the weaknesses of the church in which He wants to plant you. If you're waiting for the "perfect" church, just know it will be imperfect the moment you arrive. There is no perfect church because there are no perfect Christians.

I have heard people say, "All the people in the church are hypocrites." My reply is, "Come and join us; we can always use one more." While I certainly don't believe that everyone in the church is a hypocrite, the people who say they are Christians and refuse to gather with other believers actually practice hypocrisy. Think about it.

The benefits of gathering are great. There are promises that we are afforded and blessings that we are in line to receive. I can declare that I will flourish and blossom because I am planted, and iGather. I can declare that God will hide me in His pavilion and His tabernacle because iGather in the house of the Lord.

We need to make a commitment to gather with other believers regularly. There are great benefits, blessings, and protections afforded us as we are faithful to gather together in church. Choose today to be one who both declares and demonstrates "iGather."

CHAPTER 4

iFit

> IT IS OUR DIFFERENCE AND UNIQUENESS THAT CAUSES US TO FIT.

Now, therefore, you are no longer strangers and foreigners, but fellow citizens with the saints and members of the household of God, having been built on the foundation of the apostles and prophets, Jesus Christ Himself being the chief cornerstone, in whom the whole building, **being fitted together**, grows into a holy temple in the Lord, in whom you also are being built together for a dwelling place of God in the Spirit (Ephesians 2:19-22, emphasis added).

I believe that everyone has a desire to some degree or another to fit in. There may be some who care less if they fit; however, most human beings want to be where they fit. There is frustration produced when we feel as if we don't fit in. If we feel like the "odd ball" in the bunch, we will not stay for long.

In the previous passage of Scripture, Paul speaks of how the church is "fitted together." For the church to be fitted, the members of the church must fit. There is a place for every individual within the body of Christ. There is a place that each person within the church fits.

It is only when each member fits into their place that the church grows and is built up. Every member is needed, and every member fits. When the individuals within the church demonstrate, "iFit," the church becomes the dwelling place of God in the Spirit.

Uniqueness Makes You Fit

I can remember as a child during the Christmas season watching the animated film version of *Rudolph, the Red-Nosed Reindeer*. Rudolph was the reindeer who believed he just didn't fit in. He possessed something unique of which others poked fun: a shiny red nose. Ultimately, because of his difference, he ran away with Hermey the Elf, a toy-maker, who also felt as if he didn't fit. Hermey was supposed to be constructing toys, yet he wanted to be a dentist.

They ended up on the island of misfit toys. This island was filled with toys that believed they were defective and unwanted, and they were all sad because they believed they were misfits. These animated toys wept together in recognition of their inability to be accepted and fit in. This was always a sad and heart-breaking moment of the movie to me as a child.

Ultimately, in the end, the things that caused them to believe they didn't fit were exactly what everyone needed.

Hermey pulled out the teeth of the Abominable Snowman, and Rudolph saved Christmas by providing light to help guide the sleigh. Their uniqueness was what made them fit. The thing they possessed that was different is what made them needed by everyone else.

I recognize that Rudolph, Hermey, Santa, and the Abominable Snowman are all fictional characters. However, there are some spiritual truths that we can see demonstrated in this story. We can even say the story is a parable concerning our purpose and how we fit. Understand this principle: it is your distinct uniqueness that causes you to fit and help meet the needs of others.

Discerning and Combating the Lie

One of the tools of satan is the lie that we don't fit. He lies to Christians attempting to deceive them into believing that they don't fit anywhere. They are told by satan that they are the oddball. They are told that they are defective and should be banished to the island of misfit Christians. This is the blabbering that the enemy will pronounce. All of this is done to cause believers to separate from the people and the place where they actually fit and have purpose.

Understand this: everything that the devil says is a lie. Jesus said satan is a liar and the father of all lies (John 8:44). There is no truth in anything that the devil declares; you know he is lying because his lips are moving. It is impossible for him to tell the truth.

The fact that he would say that you don't fit means that you do. The fact that he would say that you are the

41

oddball means that you're not. The fact that he would say that you are defective means that you are fearfully and wonderfully made. The devil lies in an effort to get Christians to disconnect from those with whom God has called them to be connected. He lies to get them to stay away from the church and the people of God.

The way that we combat the enemy is with the truth of the Word of God—the sword of the Spirit. Jesus combated the enemy with the written Word of God when He was tempted. When the enemy lies to us, he attempts to manipulate us to believe something that is untrue; he tempts us with a lie.

Jesus exampled what we should do when faced with temptation by saying, "It is written." When faced with the lie that you don't fit, begin to declare, "It is written; iFit." The Word of God declares that the members of the church are "fitted together." That means iFit.

Not an Accident

I know some people have been told their entire lives that they are an accident. Children have been told that they were not planned. Sometimes they have been told that they are a mistake. While your parents may not have planned your conception, you are not an accident. God has purpose for your life. You are a member of the body of Christ, and you fit.

I constantly remind our congregation, regardless of what anyone has ever said to them, they are not an accident. Regardless of the manner in which they were conceived, they are not an accident. Regardless of their family background, they are not an accident. The Heavenly Father knew them in Christ before the foundation of the world, and they have a divine destiny and purpose.

> Just as He chose us in Him before the foundation of the world, that we should be holy and without blame before Him in love, having predestined us to adoption as sons by Jesus Christ to Himself, according to the good pleasure of His will (Ephesians 1:4-5).

This passage of Scripture declares that you were chosen in Him before the foundation of the world. That means before you were a glint in your daddy's eye, you were already chosen in Christ. You were given a divine destiny and purpose which included being a son of God. My friend, you are accepted; you are purposed; and you fit!

The next time the devil tries to tell you that you don't fit, tell him where he can go. Shout it in his face, "iFit!" Make it your daily declaration: "iFit!" Before he has a chance to say anything to you, declare "iFit!" Refuse to allow rejection to be a part of your life.

My spiritual father, Bishop Bill Hamon, said on many occasions, "If anyone draws a circle to exclude me, I draw a bigger one and include them." That's a wonderful perspective to possess! This attitude keeps rejection away. The tool of the enemy is for us to feel rejected and then reject others. We can disable that sequence by refusing to reject others when we feel as though they have rejected us. We can still say "iFit" regardless of what others may do. People do not have the ability to change the truth of God's Word because it remains forever true and cannot be changed. Therefore, I am accepted and iFit!

A Piece of the Puzzle

You should see your life, function, and ministry within a local church body like a piece of a jigsaw puzzle. No other piece looks exactly like you. Each one of us is unique in design, shape, and color combination. Each one of us fits between different pieces of the puzzle. If we are missing, the picture is incomplete. Do you get the point?

It is vital that you realize that God has made you to fit in the local church. You are like a piece of the puzzle that is needed to make the picture complete. No other piece can fill that spot but you. Why? It is because there is no other piece that will fit properly.

> Under his control all the different parts of the body fit together, and the whole body is held together by every joint with which it is provided. So when each separate part works as it should, the whole body grows and builds itself up through love (Ephesians 4:16, GNB).

I love this translation of that verse. It says that all the different parts of the body fit. I want to focus a moment on the word "different." Paul specifically says that each part is different; no two parts are exactly the same. You are an original—not a duplicate. **There aren't any clones in the body of Christ.** The truth is that you should be different because your difference is what causes you to fit.

In our church, we don't need two senior pastors. I have that position and place filled. I don't need another me. However, I do need people who possess complementary gifts and abilities to make up what I am lacking. I need pieces of the puzzle to connect with me.

The enemy has hoodwinked many believers into thinking that they must be exactly like someone else to fit. The exact opposite is the truth. You need to be the person that God created you to be with your own uniqueness. That is what gives you the ability to fit.

The balance of this truth is that we must all continually be open to adjustment. We must be willing to receive instruction and correction from the leaders whom God has placed within our lives. None of us should be renegades within the church doing things inappropriately while shouting, "I've gotta be me!" This kind of behavior is fleshly and harmful to others.

"Having then gifts differing according to the grace that is given to us, let us use them" (Romans 12:6).

Paul declares that each of us has different gifts, and we are exhorted to use those gifts. Our unique gift is designed to fit into the whole body. Your gift is there to edify and build up the body of Christ. The church will be blessed and benefited when you use your unique gifting.

No One Can Take Your Place

It seems there are some in the church who are afraid that someone will take their place. This results in them operating with a spirit of competition which leads to envy and strife and causes all sorts of problems within a church body. The reason that some operate in this manner is because they lack knowledge of the truth that no one can take their place. They are insecure because of their ignorance of the truth.

Learning to rest in the truth that there is a place for you in the church that no one else can possess will enable you to fit where you belong. You don't have to strive for recognition. You don't have to compete with someone else for your place. The gift within your life will make a place and cause you to fit. Things will fall into proper alignment when you rest in the truth that iFit.

There is no one else that will fit where you fit. You can't fit where they fit, and they can't fit where you fit. You are a unique piece of the puzzle designed by the Master Builder of the Church, Jesus. He knew what He was doing when He fashioned you. You are exactly what is needed in the place He has made you to fit.

The entire reason that iFit is because no one can take my place. The reason you can say "iFit" is because no one can take your place.

When iFit, the church is blessed. When iFit, the body of Christ is made strong. When iFit, rejection has no place in my life. When iFit, the entire church benefits, including me. Because iFit, iBelong!

CHAPTER 5

iFunction

> SATISFACTION IS THE FRUIT OF FULFILLING YOUR FUNCTION. FRUSTRATION IS THE RESULT OF FAILURE TO FUNCTION.

For I say, through the grace given to me, to everyone who is among you, not to think of himself more highly than he ought to think, but to think soberly, as God has dealt to each one a measure of faith. For as we have many members in one body, but all the members do not have the same function, so we, being many, are one body in Christ, and individually members of one another. Having then gifts differing according to the grace that is given to us, let us use them: if prophecy, let us prophesy in proportion to our faith; or ministry, let us use it in our ministering; he who teaches, in teaching; he who exhorts, in exhortation; he who gives, with liberality; he who leads, with diligence; he who shows mercy, with cheerfulness (Romans 12:3-8).

47

Every Christian is called to function within the body of Christ. There is a role that every one of us plays. Every member of a local church has their own unique function. There is something for all of us to do.

The original Greek word that is translated "function" in the above verses of Scripture is *praxis*. It means practice, work, or deed. By definition, we see the reference of a work that someone carries out. Paul is not talking about a quality or characteristic; he is talking about a work or practice. The root word means to perform repeatedly and habitually. Again, this refers to the ongoing work that is to be carried out by each individual member within the church.

Every member of the Church possesses a gift that should function within the body of Christ. The gift is not to be put on a shelf and displayed for others to see. It is given to the members of the Church for the purpose of function. Some have referred to these gifts as motivational gifts. I prefer to call them FUNCTIONAL GIFTS; they are gifts of function.

These gifts which are distributed throughout the Church are designed to function through each individual member. They don't necessarily determine what you do, but rather how you function. They are not merely personality characteristics; they are spiritual giftings that have been placed in us. Determining which gift you have will help you understand your own function. Understanding all these gifts will help you understand others.

Although an entire book could be written on these gifts, I will give a short, concise description of each of these seven functional gifts that are mentioned in the previous Scripture passage.

Seven Functional Gifts

The **first** gift mentioned is **prophecy** which is not to be confused with the gift of prophecy found in First Corinthians. The functional gift of prophecy is derived from the Greek word *propheteia*. It means to speak forth the mind and counsel of God. Those with this gifting are usually seeking the "Now Word" that God is speaking. They desire to expose and reveal what God is bringing to light. Their primary function is to flow in the supernatural gifts of the Spirit and articulate the Word of the Lord. This gift doesn't make someone a prophet, but many prophets will possess this functional gifting.

Ministry is the **second** gift mentioned. It is derived from the Greek word *diakonia* which means attendance as a servant. This gift motivates one to function as a servant within the body of Christ. Many times, they use their talents and abilities in task-oriented jobs. Their ministry function is to attend to some of the natural tasks that need to be accomplished for ministry to be fruitful. This gift is not a lesser gift; it is just different. It is a gift that is desperately needed within the body of Christ.

The gift of **teaching** is next in line. It is derived from the Greek word *didasko* which means to give instruction or inclined to preach. This functional gift enables one to teach and instruct for the purpose of bringing clarity and understanding. People with this gift are typically not as interested in supernatural manifestations as they are interested in a fresh revelation from the Word of God.

They desire exactness and a systematic presentation of truth. Many times, those with this gifting are very particular concerning semantics. They are just as concerned with how something is said as the content itself. They are usually drawn to ministries which emphasize teaching more than preaching and prophesying.

Exhortation is the **fourth** gift that is articulated. It is derived from the Greek word *perakaleo* which means to call near, to invoke, or beseech. Those who operate with this gift function as encouragers in the Church. They are like the cheerleaders of the body of Christ. Optimism and cheerfulness are common characteristics in those who possess this gift. They desire to spread joy and hope throughout the Church.

The gift of **giving** is next in line. Those with this gift believe their primary function is to "foot the bill" for the Church, and they take great joy in doing it. Many believe they are called into the business arena and are paymasters to bring wealth into the kingdom of God. Their goal is to be prosperous so that they can give in an abundant manner. Typically, they do much more financially than tithe.

The gift of **rulership** is manifested through the administration and organizational structure of the church. It functions for the purpose of establishing proper order within the body of Christ. This gift is to function "with diligence." Diligence means speed, eagerness, and businesslike. For those with this gift, they desire to see things done correctly, orderly, and excellently. They are usually agitated when things are done sloppily. People with this gift will typically demand exactness (which must be tempered).

The **last** functional gift mentioned is **mercy**. While all believers should be merciful, the gift of mercy expresses compassion and longsuffering regardless of the severity of someone's transgression. They desire to see restoration of those who have fallen and will exhibit tenderness and sympathy toward those who are in need or trouble. Their gift functions by reaching out to those who are downcast, distressed, and falling apart. They will comfort and console the hurting. They become the proverbial "shoulder to cry on" within the Church.

Different Responses to the Same Need

It is essential that we understand that no functional gift is greater than the others. All these functional gifts are important and needed within the body of Christ. Each of them possesses a unique perspective concerning the approach to ministry. Each gift is designed to function uniquely and to complement the others.

I will give you an example. There is an individual within the church that has a financial need. There is one need, but seven different responses. Here are the different ways that need would be approached.

Prophecy says, "Let's get the word of the Lord to find out what is blocking up the flow and then war a good warfare with the prophetic word."

Serving says, "How can I serve you? Can I watch your kids so you can do some extra work to make some money?"

Teaching says, "Brother, have you been renewing your mind to the Word? I'm going to agree in prayer with you according to Matthew 18:19 and believe that 3 John 2 and Philippians 4:19 will come to pass in your life. Just believe the Word, and everything will be alright."

Exhortation says, "Brother, you are going to make it! I know the answer is on the way. Don't get discouraged because I've seen God turn situations around like this before. If He did it then, He will do it again. Don't give up!"

Giving says, "How much do you need? Here is some money to take care of it."

Leadership says, "Do you have a budget? Have you been sticking to it? Bring all your financial information to me, and we will devise a plan to get you out of this mess and keep you from getting into it again."

Mercy says, "Bless your heart. I am so sorry you're having all these difficulties. I really feel what you're going through. Here, I've got fifty dollars I put back this week, but you can have it. Maybe it will help you out a little."

So, which of these responses is right? They all are right. Each of these possesses a perspective that brings a piece of the total solution to the need. All of these responses could help someone who may be in financial need.

Uniqueness and Diversity of Function

It's important to understand that each individual member of the body of Christ is unique. You are a unique member of the Church; there is no one else just like you. The Church is not comprised of spiritual clones. Instead, we are all members of one body, while being exclusive in our make-up.

Everyone in the body of Christ is different. Human tendency is to attempt to make everyone just like us. However, God loves diversity. We are all diverse in our background. We come from differing families, ethnicities, educational backgrounds, and geographical locations. However, we all share a common Father (Father God), elder brother (Jesus), and indwelling Spirit (Holy Spirit).

The nature of the kingdom of God allows for diversity. We must learn to appreciate it and embrace it. The Bible says "there are diversities of gifts." Two people can have the same gift, yet operate differently. While we share so many things in common in the church, our individual function is different.

The Balance of Diversity

Embracing diversity does not mean that we embrace compromise. When I speak of diversity, I am not speaking of tolerating sinful living. I am referring to embracing people, giftings, and functions that are not like our own.

The appreciation of diversity does not mean that you behave improperly and say, "That's just the way I am;

now, accept my diversity." The appreciation of diversity does not mean that you are free to operate outside of parameters, boundaries, and standards that are established. The appreciation of diversity does not mean that you are free to believe things that are unbiblical and not be corrected.

Glorying in "you" is not what we are referring to when speaking of diversity. That is called pride, which is sinful. That kind of attitude and disposition is idolatry. It is the exaltation and worshiping of self.

It is important to understand you are free to be "who you are" providing that transformation is taking place within your life through the renewing of your mind (Romans 12:1-2). None of us are ever free to do whatever our flesh dictates. Freedom in Christ to function as members of the body of Christ possesses boundaries and parameters which are found and articulated in the Word of God, the Bible.

Empowered to Function

We must understand that the grace of God did not liberate any of us from parameters and boundaries. Neither did it release us from the responsibility of functioning and working within the church. The grace of God actually empowers us to carry out that function with His ability and might. It enables us to do it correctly.

Many Christians have misunderstood various New Testament Scripture verses that deal with faith and works. They don't fully understand what Paul was referring to when he said that we are liberated from the works of the law. The works that Paul was referring to are not at all related to our functional work within the church. So, Paul never encouraged any believer to sit back and do nothing; it is actually the contrary. He encouraged every member of the church to function and fulfill their purpose within the body of Christ.

We were not saved merely to secure a fire insurance policy while we sit on the spiritual front porch singing "I'll Fly Away." We were saved to do something; we were saved to accomplish something while here on Earth. We all have a purpose.

The moment you were saved, your divine purpose came alive. The thing that you were created to do was resurrected and brought to life. That which you previously were unable to do was activated and ignited on the inside of you. The reason for your existence came alive.

With all of us, our reason for existence is linked to our purpose in God. Our function in the church is connected to our purpose. That purpose will involve work and productivity of some nature. It will involve putting our hand to the plow and refusing to look back. Functioning within our purpose will always involve action, work, and continual effort on our part.

Work—A Four-Letter Word

For many today, work is a nasty word. It is a four-letter word. It is a word that is avoided by many. However, every member of the church is called to work. We are all called to do something productive within the body of Christ.

It is vital to understand this simple principle: God is not lazy. He is creative and productive. We see that God created the heavens, the earth, and all living creatures in six days. It was on the seventh day that He rested. Only on one day out of seven did He sit down; He was busy creating things on the other six days. If we desire to be godly (like God), then we must embrace the truth that we are called to function. We must begin to say and demonstrate, "iFunction."

> And He Himself gave some to be apostles, some prophets, some evangelists, and some pastors and teachers, for the equipping of the saints for the work of ministry, for the edifying of the body of Christ (Ephesians 4:11-12).

Jesus has given five different ministry gifts to the church: the apostle, prophet, evangelist, pastor, and teacher. We refer to them many times as the **five-fold ministry**. These ministry gifts within the church are for the purpose of equipping believers. Well, what do they equip the believer to do? It is clearly stated in this passage of Scripture that their purpose is for the WORK of the ministry.

The five-fold ministry function within the body of Christ is to equip believers to do the work of the ministry. These ministry gifts don't do the work; rather, they equip everyday believers to accomplish the work. They equip them to function. The desire of every ministry gift in the Church should be that each member in the body of Christ can truthfully say, "iFunction."

Every Member Functioning

Many have believed for years that the work of the ministry was to be accomplished solely by the five-fold ministry. If there was anyone sick in the hospital, then it was the responsibility of the pastor to visit them. If someone needed prayer, then it was the preacher's job to pray for them. We could go on and on. Local congregations would hire pastors to do the work that needed to be done, yet be unwilling to do anything themselves. In the words of the apostle James, "These things ought not to be so" (James 3:10).

Every member in the body of Christ has a divine function. There is a work that God has for every believer to accomplish. God has something for you to do; He has a spiritual endeavor for you.

If the primary reason for salvation is so we can get to heaven, then we should all try to get there as quickly as possible. We should never go to a doctor if we are sick because it may delay our heavenly arrival. I say this sarcastically to reveal the fallacious thinking that the purpose of salvation is just to make sure someone gets to heaven.

You are saved for a purpose. You have a function in the church to accomplish. You have a divine destiny to fulfill. The moment you were saved, you were placed on the road to fulfillment. However, complete fulfillment and satisfaction will not be realized until you demonstrate the principle of "iFunction." In other words, until you are doing what you are purposed to do, there will be frustrations in your life.

The Root of Frustration

I personally believe that most all frustration is linked to being off purpose. When people do things that are not within the scope of their divine function, they will experience frustration. When our purpose goes unfulfilled, we become frustrated.

> Then the people of the land tried to discourage the people of Judah. They troubled them in building, and hired counselors against them to frustrate their purpose all the days of Cyrus king of Persia, even until the reign of Darius king of Persia (Ezra 4:4-5).

The people of Judah were assisting Zerubbabel in the rebuilding of the temple. However, the enemy stirred up the people of the land to devise a plan to stop them. So, they hired government officials to keep the people of Judah from accomplishing what they had purposed. They frustrated the people of Judah by hindering their purpose.

I believe that we can see a picture of the strategy that the devil uses to bring division and strife in the church. He attempts to keep us from fulfilling our function within the church which in turn leads to frustration. **When we fail to function, we end up frustrated.** This frustration can many times lead to murmuring, complaining, and blame-shifting. People become discontented because they are frustrated, and they are frustrated because of failure to function. The absence of function produces frustration which then produces discontentment.

Ultimately, this frustration can cause Christians to separate from one another. They can begin to feel as though they are useless and have no value. When these types of things set in, there is a domino effect of negative emotions and actions that follow. However, there is a solution; it is called iFunction!

Backsliding and Blame-shifting

In my opinion, the worst result of frustration caused by failure to function is backsliding. I've seen those who fail to function end up backsliding because they disconnected from the church. Their disconnection was simply due to the failure to function. They were unfulfilled and frustrated because their divine purpose was going undone.

The bad thing is that they didn't realize the spiritual dynamics that were taking place. They blamed others for the way they felt. They pointed their finger at others in the body of Christ (leaders in the church) and blamed them for their own failures. The reality is that once people begin to point a finger, they sabotage the remedy for their situation. Pointing the finger has never produced anything other than getting kicked out of the Garden of Eden.

Adam blamed the only two people he knew when God confronted him. He said, "The WOMAN that YOU gave

59

me." He accepted no responsibility. He blamed the only people he knew, Eve and God. Think about it.

Frustration is never a reason to blame others for one's own failure to function. The responsibility to function can only be assumed by one person; that person is you. You must assume the responsibility to get connected, stay connected, and then function. Don't allow petty offenses to keep you from doing what God purposed for you to do!

Much of the previously mentioned turmoil is eliminated when church members are activated and moving in their gifts and anointing. When people find their purpose and then function within it, there is peace and fulfillment. When believers begin to function in the manner that God has purposed, it causes them to feel and say, "iBelong."

Created with a Purpose and Function

"Then the LORD God took the man and put him in the garden of Eden to tend and keep it" (Genesis 2:15).

After God created Adam, He placed him in a place of total perfection, the Garden of Eden. There was a divine purpose for man being placed there which is clearly articulated in the above passage of Scripture: Adam was to tend and keep the garden. Adam's purpose meant he would be required to function.

The Hebrew word translated "tend" means to work and to serve. So, we see that God purposed for Adam to actually work. He was not merely to wander around naked all day throughout the garden. God's original plan was not an eternal vacation for man. Adam had an assignment; he had a purpose. Adam had a function to carry out in the Garden of Eden.

One of the first things that God did after creating Adam was to give him a function. God gave Adam a job. He gave him something productive to do with his time. Adam was given an occupation. God did not create man to sit around all day in a recliner at home to watch television. God did not create the couch potato. He created a man with a function.

We clearly see that God placed Adam in the garden to be productive. We need to understand that God desires for us to be productive believers. We are in the kingdom of God to produce good fruit. In serving the Lord, there will be productivity as we function within our purpose.

Adam did more than just commune with the Lord in the cool of the evening. His purpose was more than merely fellowshipping with his creator. While it was an important part of his day, the majority of the day was taken up with his function. Adam did not spend his day only communing with the Lord; he had a job. Adam worked. Adam had a function.

My personal opinion is that one of the things that caused the fall of Adam and Eve was a failure to function. They were distracted from their purpose by illegitimate things. Lounging around the tree that produced fruit which God had forbidden them to eat was not in Adam or Eve's job description. Carrying on a conversation with a lying serpent was not fulling the purpose of God. When Adam and Eve were distracted from their function is when they fell. Getting Adam and Eve off purpose was a tactic that the devil used to cause the fall of man. Think about it.

There are some in the church today who are hungry for the Word of God and the move of the Holy Spirit, yet don't want to work in any area of church ministry. While I commend them for their hunger, it must be stated that God never called any of us to "live in the glory" while we ignore the work that is to be done.

Some have used the story of Mary and Martha as an excuse for pursuing God's presence while forgetting about the work. However, even in that particular account, it was only a short moment of time that Mary wasn't working. I personally believe you can do both. You can pursue the glory of God and still function at the same time. You can pursue everything that God has for you spiritually, yet still work and fulfill your purpose. We don't have to pit one thing against the other. Pursuit and work can dwell and operate together; you can function and go after His presence at the same time.

Hippie Christianity

In the 1960s, there was a group of people that became known as Hippies. For the most part, they were an anti-establishment group that rebelled against just about everything in society. They rebelled against the institution of marriage with the promotion of "free-love." They rebelled against their employers and the economic establishment by being homeless, sleeping wherever they could find a place to lay their head, and eating whatever they could find or steal. They practiced lawlessness and spoke negatively of police officials and authorities.

Unfortunately, after some of the "Hippies" received Jesus, they brought many of the same attitudes and philosophies of the Hippie Movement into the Church. Many of them became involved in the Jesus Movement that took place in the late 1960s and early 1970s. Much of this was nothing more than a Christianized version of the Hippie Movement. Rebellion and lawlessness continued to be practiced.

There are still some believers who have adopted that same spirit and brought it into the Church. They practice lawlessness. They refuse to be married to a local church body—floating from church to church. They speak negatively of church leaders. They consider legitimate biblical parameters and boundaries as man-made rules that seek to quench their fire.

Many times, these believers will do nothing within the church in the way of working. They see the moving of the Holy Spirit much like the Hippies saw smoking marijuana and taking psychedelic drugs. They live for the moment and the experience rather than living to be productive through functioning. Their primary motivation becomes the feeling and thrill of the moment rather than long term fruit produced as the result of being a stable and constant believer.

Here is an important principle that you should commit to memory: **we do not live for a momentary experience; we live to function and fulfill our purpose.** It is only when we function that we see divine purpose fulfilled. We are called to accomplish something within the kingdom of God. This will happen when we function in the manner that God has called and anointed us.

Perfection Not Required

Perfection is not a prerequisite of functioning within the Church. Many believers fail to function because they believe they have not arrived at a place of sinless living or holiness that would merit them functioning at any level. While I believe in the importance of living a holy life, function within the local church is not predicated on total sinless living. If that were the requirement, there would be no one in the church who could function.

Jesus chose twelve men to be His disciples who later became the twelve apostles (Judas excluded). All of them possessed certain issues in their lives. Peter was impetuous, foul-mouthed, and fearful; he spouted off when he should have been quiet. Peter conducted himself improperly on numerous occasions and possessed issues of racism and people-pleasing that produced hypocrisy in his life. However, Peter still functioned in the Church.

On the Day of Pentecost, Peter preached, and 3000 people were saved and added to the church. He healed the lame man that was laid daily at the gate to ask for alms. His shadow was attributed to healing many who were sick and diseased. Also, he was the only disciple to ever walk on water. Peter wasn't perfect, but he still functioned.

You don't have to wait to be perfect to start functioning. God will use you just like you are. He will begin to mold you into His image as you are faithful to step out and use your gift. That gift will grow and develop as you do.

You Learn by Doing

I can remember when I was first asked to lead worship over 35 years ago. I was a trained musician (a trumpet major in college and piano minor). However, I was not a good vocalist, and I had difficulty doing two things at the same time. In worship leading, you are actually doing about three things at the same time, if you play an instrument simultaneously.

There was no one else at the church that could lead worship, so I was asked to do so. I said, "Yes." **On a side note, your purpose and destiny will always be fulfilled on the other side of your "Yes!"** When I first started leading worship, it was overwhelming to me. I was playing, singing, leading the worship team, and exhorting the congregation all at the same time.

Since I was a trained musician, but not a trained vocalist, I could hear notes I sang that were off pitch (out of tune). I could not seem to make my voice sing it correctly. In my mind I thought, "These poor people have to listen to me sing." However, I kept working at it until I got better. The more I did it, the better I got.

Later on, I began writing worship songs. Many of these songs were recorded by Integrity Music™. I eventually led worship on one of their worship recordings, *Hosanna 28—Victor's Crown*, and over a quarter of a million copies were sold. My voice and songs traveled around the world as a result. Who would have ever thought it? I certainly didn't when I started out leading worship for thirty people in a storefront church.

Understand this principle: **you learn by doing**. No one learns to swim by merely watching swimming events at the Olympics. They learn to swim by getting in the water. If you don't jump in, you will never learn to swim.

There is only one way to learn to function in your gift and anointing, and that is to jump in. You must "take the plunge." Like a diver on a diving board, you just have to do it!

Jesus said that He is the vine, and we are the branches (John 15:1-2). He continued to say that every branch that did not bear fruit is removed and carried away. The branches that refuse to function and fulfill their purpose will be removed from their place. In other words, if we do not function, He will raise up someone else to take the place that we vacate. While no one can take our place, if we fail to function, God will raise up somebody else to fulfill that purpose. I don't want that to happen in my life, and I'm sure your sentiments are the same. Therefore, iFunction!

Have Some Fun

Our approach to our function within the church determines whether we will enjoy it or dread it. It's interesting that the first three letters of function spell FUN. I believe we can have fun while we FUN-ction. It is not drudgery; it is life-giving. It is spiritually stimulating when we FUN-ction.

That's part of the reason the Psalmist said, "I was glad when they said unto me, 'Let us go to the house of the Lord'" (Psalm 122:1). He didn't say he was sad; he said he was glad. You can be glad because you go to the house of the Lord to FUN-ction.

You can have a blast functioning if you have the right attitude. Take upon yourself the attitude that your function in the church is needed by others because IT IS! Take upon yourself the disposition that whatever I do and however iFunction, I am doing this unto the Lord. Jesus said, "[If you] have done it unto one of the least of these my brethren, [you] have done it unto me" (Matthew 25:40, KJV).

You have a function. When you function, you will sense that you belong. You are not an accident, and you have a supernatural purpose that needs to be accomplished as you function. Make this declaration over your life daily: "iFunction to fulfill my purpose because iBelong."

CHAPTER 6

iEngage

> BELIEVERS MUST ENGAGE WITH OTHER BELIEVERS. THIS IS NOT SOMETHING THAT CAN BE SUCCESSFULLY DONE OVER THE INTERNET, FACETIME, OR VIDEO CONFERENCING. WHILE THOSE THINGS MAY ASSIST, BELIEVERS NEED TO GATHER TOGETHER AND ENGAGE WITH ONE ANOTHER FACE TO FACE AND HEART TO HEART.

Anything in which you involve yourself should be done with an "all-in" philosophy. Paul said that whatever we do should be done as unto the Lord. I can't imagine any believer doing something half-heartedly for Jesus. When Jesus went to the cross for us, He didn't do it half-heartedly; Jesus was "all-in." He was fully engaged. Likewise, we should be fully engaged in the body of Christ. Since iBelong, iEngage.

Trained athletes can have everything in their body working optimally; every muscle can be working at its peak. However, just one muscle seizing up in a moment of time can disable that athlete. One part of their body that can no longer engage in the task at hand will cripple them.

We need to understand the importance of engaging in the local church which means full involvement of our being:

spirit, soul, and body. It means that we are willing to give of ourselves. It means prioritizing the things of God and His house. It means freeing ourselves from distractions that would keep us from being engaged in the kingdom of God.

In the world today, there are so many things that can distract us. The devil uses distraction to keep us from fulfilling our destiny and purpose in God. He uses distraction to blind us to the things that are the most important. It is distraction that prevents many believers from doing the will of God.

Engaging in a church body begins with faithful attendance. We have already shared on this principle in the chapter entitled "iGather." The truth is that your engagement will be very limited if you're not there. You cannot engage with the people of God if you elect to excuse yourself from their presence. Attendance is required for you to engage with others in the local church.

The Need for Human Touch

I recognize that social media outlets allow people to connect with others, but nothing will ever take the place of human touch. It has been proven scientifically that human beings need human touch to survive. We were not created to be loners living in individualized protective bubbles; we were created to engage with others in the church.

The importance of human touch cannot be overstated. Jesus touched people when He walked the face of this earth. He touched lepers, the sick and infirmed, the afflicted and possessed, and at one time touched a coffin. Some of these things were unlawful to do. The lady with the issue of blood pressed through the crowd to touch the hem of Jesus' garment. Jesus laid His hands upon people who needed healing and a touch from God.

All humans need human touch. Most human beings desire and crave human touch. It is rare that any human being despises being touched by another person. Why is this phenomenon real? It is because God created us to need one another. We were not designed to be alone. Neither were we designed to live without being touched.

Just like we need food to survive, we need human touch. As food provides nourishment and strength for our natural bodies, so touch provides nourishment, encouragement, and tranquility for the emotional aspect of man. A loving touch from another person has amazing positive effects on human beings.

Created to Experience Touch

When a man and woman begin to court one another, it is not unusual to see them holding hands. People do not hold hands to proclaim to the world their romantic feelings toward one another. They do this because they desire to feel the touch of the person's hand they are holding. They will embrace one another because their feelings of love toward each other can be communicated through touching. They want to feel nearness and belonging that comes through physical human touch.

When my wife and I dated each other, I held her hand. I would also hug her. Later on, we kissed one another. After we were married, the touching was more intimate. Four years into our marriage we had our first child. This happened because of an intimate physical relationship that involved touching one another. It didn't happen because of a long-term relationship on Facebook® or any other social media outlet. We didn't tweet one another to have a baby.

Dangers of Electronic Replacement

More and more people are turning to electronic media for everything in their life. We now have video school, video conferencing, video training, electronic church on the web, etc. These things are not inherently evil. However, when they become a substitute for the real, they become dangerous. When we take human touch out of the equation, we are erasing something God said is needed.

In our society today, many people have replaced human touch with the internet and social media. A recent survey found that young men are finding real women less desirable sexually because their sexual desires are being fulfilled through internet pornography (which is sinful). Many people have replaced human touch with a counterfeit. Ultimately, those who do such things will crash.

Today, parents and their children are texting each other while living in the same house. We seem to be more connected than ever, while we are less involved and less engaged with one another overall. Loneliness has become an epidemic in spite of all the social media outlets available.

I'm not coming against all of our electronic technology. However, we have lost something important in our age of connectivity. We have lost sight of the fact that HUMANS NEED TOUCH. God created us that way.

No one is exempt or excluded from needing to be touched; we all need it. From the time a baby is born, they need human touch. Most of the time, when a baby is born, it is placed on its mother's chest. There is bonding that begins the moment a baby touches its mother. The baby feels secure, and its crying is hushed as it feels the comforting touch of its mother.

The Touch of God—Josiah's Story

In August of 2009, the Holy Spirit led me to minister a message entitled *"The Touch of God."* While I believe that we are to walk by faith and not by sight or feelings, I also believe we need to experience the touch of God. There is nothing wrong with desiring to feel His presence. While my faith is not moved by what I feel, it is reassuring to feel His power, presence, and anointing.

In preparation for that message, I did a tremendous amount of research on human touch. I had never researched this before. I was surprised at what I found to be scientifically proven concerning touch. That information was interwoven in my message. I didn't realize at the time the importance of the research that I had conducted.

A few weeks later, on August 23rd, our first grandson, Josiah Robert Gay, was born (son of our oldest son, Joshua). He was born six weeks premature with a full knot in the umbilical cord. It was also wrapped around his neck three times, he was not breathing, and there was no heartbeat; he was stillborn.

My wife, Stacey, was in the delivery room and was texting me a play-by-play rundown of all the things that were transpiring while I waited with family and friends. My wife texted me, "He's not breathing; we need him to breathe." He had not breathed for over two minutes at that time. The nurses said, "Two minutes, still." I immediately texted back, "IN JESUS NAME, BREATHE!" The text came through on my wife's phone with a "ding." Immediately, Josiah let out his first cry.

My wife came running out of the delivery room and into the waiting room. She shouted, "He breathed; He breathed!" She was crying as we embraced and then she collapsed in my arms. We both cried together. We all rejoiced and wept. God resurrected our grandson, and our faith prevailed.

While we were rejoicing that Josiah was breathing, there was still a battle that was being fought. He only weighed four pounds and was six weeks premature. His lungs were not fully developed, and he did not get the final rush of blood into his system that usually comes through the umbilical cord during normal birthing with no complications. He was anemic and had no strength.

They rushed him to the Newborn Intensive Care Unit (NICU). The nurse told our son and daughter-in-law,

"You have a very sick little boy." They went on to say that he would be in the NICU for at least six weeks. They said that he would have breathing issues. They said he would possibly have some disabilities because of the length of time without oxygen to the brain. There were also other things they said he would suffer as the result of the complications at birth. He scored a one on his Apgar score which is the lowest a newborn can receive and still be alive. The medical fact is that less than one percent of babies that are born vaginally with a full knot in their umbilical cord survive. Viability is virtually impossible when they are born prematurely with a full knot.

When we heard that he was going to be in the NICU for a long time, the message I had preached on the touch of God arose in my heart. I felt we needed to have people around Josiah 24/7 in the NICU. With his parents, Joshua and Miranda, my wife Stacey and I, along with his maternal grandparents, we established a schedule where one of us would be in the NICU with him round the clock.

Josiah was in an incubator, but we sat right beside the incubator and reached our hands in and touched his little fingers. We would speak to him the promise of God. I can remember singing to him and worshiping the Lord as I would touch him. We did this for six days.

On day three of his stay in the NICU, he reached up and pulled the feeding tube out of his nose. The doctor asked the nurses, "Who took the tube out?" They told him that they didn't do it. He replied, "Well, I guess he didn't like it and doesn't need it anymore." Throughout his stay, he surprised the medical professionals because he was progressing at a pace that wasn't supposed to happen.

At the end of the sixth day and the beginning of the seventh, August 30th (his father's birthday), Josiah was released from the NICU. He went into a regular room at the hospital with his mother, Miranda. On the tenth day from his birth, he went home.

The medical professionals said he would be there for at least six weeks. They said he would have all sorts of issues. However, God resurrected, restored, and healed him. Today, he is a healthy young man with absolutely none of the issues declared that he would possess. Hallelujah! God is faithful!

The reason I share this story is because of the element of touch that played such a vital role in his recovery. I believe God healed Josiah. However, spiritual principles and dynamics that God created and instituted were instrumental in producing and accelerating that healing process. We were continually touching him. While in the NICU, we rarely saw any other people there except for the nurses. Most of the babies were there alone with no one to touch them or speak to them. Our hearts broke for them.

Science Proves Humans Need Physical Touch

The scientific research is now overwhelming that humans need touch to survive. Science has proven that the brain releases and withholds certain chemicals that regulate the physical and emotional development of infants. The actions of the brain are significantly influenced by touch. Research reveals that premature infants who experience gentle stroking for just 45 minutes a day after ten days weigh 47% heavier than those who are not. These babies also exhibit a happier disposition. They are more active, alert, and responsive.

Here is some information that you will find interesting and enlightening.

> Scientists have shown that the amount of body contact in our lives plays a vital role in our mental and physical development as infants and in our happiness and vigor as adults. Touch influences our ability to deal with stress and pain, to form close relationships with other people, and even to fight off disease.

> Various studies have shown that when someone else gently holds a person's wrist, heartbeat slows and blood pressure declines. Children and adolescents, hospitalized for psychiatric problems, show remarkable reductions in anxiety levels and positive changes in attitude when they receive a brief daily back rub. The arteries of rabbits fed a high-cholesterol diet and petted regularly had 60% fewer blockages than did the arteries of un-petted but similarly fed rabbits. ("The Healing Power of Touch for Disease, Well-Being & Aging," http://foreverhealthyblogspot.com/2012/04/healing-power-of-touch-for-disease-well.html).

Please understand that the purpose of this book is not to give a science lesson. However, we can observe a spiritual principle that science has proven to be true. God said it in the beginning, "It is not good for man to be alone." We need one another, and we need His touch and human touch. Therefore, we must engage with each other.

Believers must engage with other believers. This is not something that can be successfully done over the internet, Facetime®, or video conferencing. While those things may assist, believers need to gather together and engage with one another face-to-face and heart-to-heart.

Jesus physically laid hands on people. There's only one example that we have where Jesus just spoke the Word for someone to be healed. However, Jesus had physical contact with the centurion who told him to speak the word only. We see that the centurion still engaged with Jesus. The bottom line is that the centurion had to engage with Jesus before the Word could be spoken and his servant healed. Engaging with one another is an essential principle for successful progression in the purpose and plan of God for our lives.

Open Your Ears

Another important way that we engage with others is through listening. It is important to listen closely to what is being taught and ministered from the pulpit. No one should go to church merely for religious obligation. Engaging and connecting to the pastor of a local church body requires that you hear his heart. Being there only to "clock-in" another Sunday in church is not the path to connection. Opening your ears to hear and receive will cause a genuine heart connection.

Jesus talked about the importance of hearing:

"Having eyes, do you not see? And having ears, do you not hear? And do you not remember?" (Mark 8:18).

Jesus said that even though you have eyes, you can still be blind. He said that even though you have ears, you can still be deaf. Seeing and hearing are what happens when we choose to engage. While you can audibly hear syllables coming out of someone's mouth, you still cannot hear and perceive what they say unless you engage. Jesus emphasized the importance of engaging in the process of hearing.

You must connect with the one who is ministering and what is being preached for it to become a part of your life. You cannot passively listen to the Word being preached and expect it to have a positive effect on your life. That is not engaging with the Word. For the Word to produce in your life, you must engage and connect.

There have been times in my life where my wife has said something to me while I was looking directly at her. I heard syllables come out of her mouth but comprehended nothing because my mind was distracted at the time. Obviously, she was not happy when I asked her to repeat herself. The reality is that I heard syllables come out of her mouth, but nothing registered in my brain because I was not engaged at the moment. Perhaps you have experienced something similar.

The Pharisees heard with their natural ears everything that Jesus taught. However, they never heard because they never engaged and connected with Jesus. They stood afar off and were distracted by the religious traditions of men and false doctrines created to appease a backslidden people. They could only find fault with all that Jesus taught because they never engaged and connected with Him.

Disengaging Causes Forfeited Blessing

When people disconnect and disengage from a pastor or minister within a church, they will begin to find fault with everything they say. What ministered life to them in previous months will then become stale manna. The reality is the pastor didn't change. Rather, the individual disengaged and disconnected.

There have been people who have come into our church and said, "This is the greatest church I've ever attended. Pastor Robert, I am with you, and you can count on me." They would come for a season of time and sit near the front of the church while engaging in the messages being delivered from the pulpit. They would give a hearty amen to truths that would resonate within them.

Six months later, they moved to the back of the auditorium. They no longer entered in during worship and acted disinterested the entire time the Word was being preached. Please hear this: nothing changed except their hearts. They stopped engaging in the ministry that was being brought forth. They disconnected from the pastor and the church. While their bodies occupied a chair, their hearts were not there.

If you disconnect a lamp from an electrical outlet, it will not illuminate. If you disengage a car's transmission, it will go nowhere. If you choose to disconnect from the message being preached, you will forfeit the blessing that message will produce within your life. If you disconnect from the pastor and church, you will miss out on the benefits that both of them bring.

I regularly encourage our congregation to engage in the ministry of the Word which means they turn on their ears. It means they clear themselves of distractions. It means that they forget about what's for lunch. It means they fully and wholly give their undivided attention to the Word that is being preached at that moment.

Revelation knowledge will always flow to those who engage. It cannot flow to those who are disconnected. When we hear the Word, we must listen with an asserted posture.

Ears On—Phone Off

It has become common for people to possess smartphones; I have one myself. They are tremendous tools. There is hardly anything that you can't do today with a smartphone. You can shop, research, view, and purchase just about anything under the sun with a smartphone or tablet. It's amazing.

Unfortunately, many believers are distracted in church services by their smartphones. They stare at it, surf the internet, look at their Facebook® feed, and tweet all during the preaching of the Word. As a result, they receive nothing. They go home unchanged. The Word that is sent to liberate them passes over them because they fail to engage. There is a continual forfeiting of blessing because of failure to connect.

While I understand that many have Bible apps on their smartphones, it is a great idea to put up your smartphone when in church. If you are easily distracted by the internet and social media, it would be a good idea for you to turn your phone off or leave it in your automobile. It is difficult to engage in the service when distracted by your phone. Sometimes it's not smart to be on your smartphone. Selah.

We can only receive from other members of the body of Christ when we engage. Blessing will flow to us when we engage. The Pharisees failed to engage in the ministry of Jesus; the distractions of their religious traditions and doctrines of men caused a disconnectedness. They were unable to receive from Jesus because they failed to engage.

We should all learn a lesson from the Pharisees contrasted with Jesus' disciples. The Pharisees were disconnected and distracted while Jesus' disciples were connected and engaged. Distractions will cause you to forfeit blessing while engaging will produce life. If you want blessing and life, then choose to engage. I desire blessing and life, so iEngage!

iFlow

> THE BAPTISM IN THE HOLY SPIRIT IS THE DOORWAY FOR RIVERS OF LIVING WATER TO FLOW THROUGH YOU. IT IS THE DOORWAY TO THE SUPERNATURAL POWER AND MANIFESTATION OF THE HOLY SPIRIT.

On the last day, that great day of the feast, Jesus stood and cried out, saying, "If anyone thirsts, let him come to Me and drink. He who believes in Me, as the Scripture has said, out of his heart will flow rivers of living water." But this He spoke concerning the Spirit, whom those believing in Him would receive; for the Holy Spirit was not yet given, because Jesus was not yet glorified (John 7:37-39).

This passage of Scripture is one that is familiar to most Spirit-filled believers. Jesus spoke of a river of life-giving water that would flow forth after the Holy Spirit was sent. He was prophesying of what would be released on the Day of Pentecost. He spoke of the experience we call the baptism in the Holy Spirit (also referred to as the infilling of the Holy Spirit).

This experience is subsequent to salvation and empowers believers to do the works of Jesus. It empowers believers to lay hands on the sick and see them recover. The baptism in the Holy Spirit is the endowment of the same power that Jesus experienced as He walked the face of this earth.

This infilling is available to every believer. No one has been left out. If you are saved, you are a candidate. If you have confessed Jesus as your Lord, you are a candidate. If you have been washed in the blood, you can receive the infilling of the Holy Spirit.

My Testimony

I received the baptism in the Holy Spirit when I was eleven years old. I went to a youth meeting on a Tuesday night. My parents dropped me off at the church where the service was being held. To this day, I cannot remember anything that happened in the service other than what happened to me and the events that led up to my experience.

The youth leader gave an invitation for those who had not received the baptism in the Holy Spirit. He said, "If you don't have the baptism, then we want to pray for you to get it." As an eleven-year-old boy, I didn't know what "the baptism" looked like. I wasn't totally sure about what the youth leader was talking. I was raised in a Pentecostal church, yet had limited knowledge of the baptism in the Holy Spirit. I had previously heard people speak in tongues but had no idea I could receive the infilling of the Holy Spirit and do the same.

Some people came up for prayer in response to the invitation of the youth leader. As they did, others within the youth group would gather around them and begin to pray. The youth leader said, "Let's all gather around and pray for them." One by one they began to pray for those who responded.

As they prayed, I came up in the very back of the pack and laid my hand on a large lady. Since I was unsure of everything transpiring, I felt I could hide behind her and not be seen. When the praying would become intense, she would shake all over. Well, I thought that was what you were supposed to do. So, when she would shake, I would shake (almost like a cold chill running down your spine).

Then to my surprise, she turned around and looked at me and announced to everyone there, "Brother Dale, I believe that this little boy can get the baptism." With no chance to respond, I was immediately pulled up to the front as hands came from all directions to be laid on me as I received prayer to "get the baptism."

They began to pray intensely for me to be baptized in the Holy Spirit. There were people saying "hold on," while others were saying "turn loose." You have to understand that in those days (early 1970s), in most Pentecostal churches, there was no instruction given as how to receive the baptism in the Holy Spirit other than the things people would shout out as they were praying for you. They would just pray and keep praying until something happened.

I lifted up my hands to heaven and began to praise and worship the Lord. I began to cry out to God to receive what they called "the baptism." I really didn't fully know what to expect. Then suddenly, in the middle of all the commotion, something began to bubble up from my spirit-man. Then words began to come out of my mouth that I did not know and had never uttered. I received the baptism in the Holy Spirit, and I spoke in tongues as the Spirit gave me utterance. The same thing that happened on the day of Pentecost 2000 years ago, happened to me as an eleven-year-old boy.

Every time I opened my mouth, a heavenly language would come out. To speak a word in English, I had to concentrate heavily and make myself speak. My mother picked me up and asked how the meeting went. I made myself say, "Good." I believe that was the only word I said for the entire trip home. I went straight to bed. I prayed in tongues until I fell asleep. Tongues had become my new language.

That was a life-changing event that happened to me. I still remember events from that night vividly. God released something within me that initiated a life-giving river of spiritual water. That river is still flowing today. However, the river has gotten bigger—larger and greater in expanse—because the more you let it flow, the greater it grows.

Today, I know much more than what I knew when I was an eleven-year-old boy at a youth meeting. Since then, we have learned how to properly instruct people to receive the infilling of the Holy Spirit. As a result, more people receive and speak in tongues.

Doorway to the Supernatural

The infilling of the Holy Spirit is the doorway to the supernatural power of God. While salvation translates you into the kingdom of God, the infilling of the Holy Spirit equips and empowers you to function in the kingdom of God. It empowers you to do all that Jesus spoke of in the sixteenth chapter of Mark. Jesus said that you would cast out devils, speak in tongues, and lay hands on the sick and see them recover. He said that these were signs that would follow and accompany those who believe (Mark 16:17-18).

The reality is that you cannot fully function like Jesus in the earth until a flow has been initiated within your life. Until the power of the Holy Spirit is flowing through you, it is impossible to do what Jesus did. Jesus didn't perform any miracle solely because He was the Son of God. He performed them because He was anointed of the Holy Spirit.

> How God anointed Jesus of Nazareth with the Holy Spirit and with power, who went about doing good and healing all who were oppressed by the devil, for God was with Him (Acts 10:38).

Even though Jesus was the Son of God, He divested himself of His deity when He came to earth. He became a man in the likeness of sinful flesh; however, Jesus never sinned. He overcame it all through the power of the Holy Spirit and the spoken Word of God.

We see in the above passage of Scripture that Jesus was anointed with the Holy Spirit and power. The word "power" is translated from the Greek word *dunamis*, meaning miracle-working power. Then, before Jesus ascended to heaven, He told His disciples that they would receive that same power (*dunamis*) after the Holy Spirit came upon them.

The Same Spirit and Same Power

It was the same power (*dunamis*) and same Holy Spirit that Jesus possessed that was made available to the disciples. It is the same power and same Holy Spirit that is available to you and me now. The same miracle-working power that operated within the life of Jesus as He walked the face of this earth is released in our lives at the moment we receive the baptism in the Holy Spirit. It is the same power and the same Spirit.

The Holy Spirit and His power constitute the river that Jesus spoke of when He said that "out of your heart (belly) will flow rivers of living water." Jesus was declaring that the baptism in the Holy Spirit is designed to be a flow in your life. It is designed to flow to others to bring healing, deliverance, and restoration.

Flowing River vs. Stagnated Pond

Rivers are designed to flow and move. Any river that stops flowing becomes stagnate. Many believers become spiritually stagnate because they stop flowing or they have never had a Holy Spirit flow initiated. There are many believers that become a dead sea because nothing is flowing in or out of their lives. This is not God's plan.

Spiritual stagnation in the lives of believers is caused by the shutdown of the flow of the Holy Spirit. Churches become stagnate when they disallow the flow of the Holy Spirit. As a result, entertainment is substituted for the anointing and power of the Holy Spirit. Emotional excitement replaces the presence of God. Where there is no flow of the Holy Spirit, people will look for a substitute. However, there is nothing that can replace the flow of the Holy Spirit within a church body.

In Paul's letter to the Corinthians, he spoke of nine manifestation gifts that the Holy Spirit would release within the church.

> But the manifestation of the Spirit is given to each one for the profit of all: for to one is given the word of wisdom through the Spirit, to another the word of knowledge through the same Spirit, to another faith by the same Spirit, to another gifts of healings by the same Spirit, to another the working of miracles, to another prophecy, to another discerning of spirits, to another different kinds of tongues, to another the interpretation of tongues. But one and the same Spirit works all these things, distributing to each one individually as He wills (1 Corinthians 12:7-11).

These nine gifts are broken up into three categories: revelation gifts, utterance gifts, and power gifts. The **revelation gifts** are the word of knowledge, word of wisdom, and discerning of spirits. **Utterance gifts** include the gift of tongues, interpretation of tongues, and prophecy. The **power gifts** are made up of the gifts of healings, working of miracles, and the gift of faith.

There have been many books written that discuss these gifts in detail and how they manifest. I will not take the time to elaborate. I desire for you to have the basic understanding that these gifts are given by the Holy Spirit to flow within the church to profit the body of Christ. They are not strange or peculiar. It should be the established norm in churches that these gifts are regularly in operation. There should be freedom for them to flow within the church.

We Need Prophecy

Many years ago, I was a guest speaker for a praise and worship conference. There were other speakers there also. One of the speakers, while in the pulpit, threw down his Bible on the platform and said, "You don't need a prophecy, you already have a book full of prophecy." He said it as a derogatory comment toward those who would desire to receive a prophecy and the operation of that gift within the church.

As I sat there, I began to think, "Well, the written Word is where I see the necessity of prophecy." The book of prophecy that He referred to (the Bible) says that we need the gift of prophecy in operation. It declares that it should flow within the church. The apostle Paul went so far as to say, "Covet to prophesy" (1 Corinthians 14:39, KJV).

So, why would Paul, by the unction and direction of the Holy Spirit, exhort us to covet to prophesy if it was unneeded? The obvious answer is he commanded us to covet it because we need the function and flow of prophecy in the church! There is nothing that God placed and ordained within the church that we don't need. We need it all!

Many believers don't understand that statements which diminish the importance of spiritual gifts flowing in the church are statements of arrogance. If we say we don't need what God instituted in the church, we are declaring that we know more than God. If God instituted it, then we need it! We need the flow of the Holy Spirit. We need His gifts in manifestation.

For there to be a flow of the Holy Spirit, there must be a vessel that He can flow through. As was stated previously, the baptism in the Holy Spirit is the doorway for rivers of living water to flow through you. It is the doorway to the supernatural power and manifestation of the Holy Spirit. It initiates and makes way for the flow of the Holy Spirit to be generated through your life and ministry.

Follow the Pattern

In February of 1988, I was ordained by Bishop Bill Hamon. During my ordination, he prophesied to me, "You will stand and prophesy by the hour." At that time, the most I had ever prophesied was maybe five minutes. I knew that I had prophetic and revelatory giftings, but I didn't totally understand at the time how to fully activate, release, and flow in those giftings. I was in the process of learning.

It just so happened that three days following my ordination, I was scheduled to give my testimony at the Full Gospel Businessmen meeting held in Panama City Beach, Florida. The president of that chapter, Gene Ford, was a regular attendee of the Friday Night School of the Holy Spirit that was conducted at Christian International where I was the worship leader. It was typical to have prophetic ministry every Friday night in those services. At the end of the service, Bishop Hamon would invite certain ministers on staff to come onto the platform. I was one of those who would minister from time to time. We would believe God for a flow of the Holy Spirit that would minister to those in attendance. We would call people out of the congregation and prophesy to them as the Holy Spirit directed.

Since Brother Ford went to those Friday night meetings and saw how the experienced prophets flow, he assumed that I was able to do the same. So, after my testimony was complete at the meeting, to my total surprise, he said to all the men there, "If there is anyone that needs a prophetic word, just line up here on my left and Brother Robert will minister to you."

When I heard this, I was in shock and disbelief; he had not discussed this with me at all. The first thing that came to my mind was, "WHAT did you say?" Then a bit of panic hit me as I realized he had just volunteered me to do something I had never done before. There was a spiritual S.O.S. signal being offered up while I smiled at everyone.

As I began to cry out to God silently, I heard the Lord say, "Follow the pattern." Immediately my mind began to rehearse everything that I had seen Bishop Hamon do over the last two months that I had been on staff at Christian International. That's not a long time to learn. However, I began to recall how the personal ministry transpired in those meetings.

Step by Step

In my mind, I slowly went through every step I saw Bishop Hamon do when he would prophesy to someone. Step **one** was he laid hands on their head. So, I laid hands on their head. Step **two** was he would pray a particular prayer that went something like this: "Father, we don't know anything about this person, but you know all things. You said that the secret things belong to the Lord, so we ask that you reveal those secret things you desire to be spoken, in Jesus name." Although that is not the exact prayer word for word, it is what I remembered. So, I prayed that prayer.

Step **three** was that Bishop Hamon would pray over them in tongues forcefully while rocking their head back and forth. So, I did the same thing. I made sure to do it because I heard the Lord say, "Follow the pattern." I wasn't going to leave anything undone, so I rocked their head back and forth and prayed in tongues while I did it.

The **fourth** step was that he would say, "Hmm, Hmm, Hmm." So, I did that too. I was committed to following the pattern I had seen demonstrated. Every person that came to receive ministry heard, "Hmm, Hmm, Hmm."

The **last** step Bishop Hamon did was to declare, "For the Lord would say," and then declare what was bubbling up by the Holy Ghost. Well, much to my surprise, the pattern worked. I stood there for almost two hours and prophesied to everyone until there was no one else remaining. A river began to flow out of my spirit man as I stirred up the gift within me. Praise God that we can follow those who through faith and patience inherit the promises (Hebrews 6:12). Biblical patterns will work if we will only work them.

The Holy Spirit initiated a flow within me—a life-giving river—that is still in operation today. Now, I have prophesied to multitudes of people. The river that the Holy Spirit initiated has only grown wider, larger, and greater in magnitude and power.

Many believers fail to understand principles concerning growing in the things of the Spirit. They understand growing in the Word, but not growing in the Spirit. It is essential to realize that your spiritual giftings can grow and develop in the same way that an athlete can develop abilities in the natural. The Bible says we "grow in grace." "Grace" is the Greek word *charis* which is the root word for "charisma" which means gift or gifting. Therefore, we grow in our gift and gifting.

Given to Every Man

The previous Scripture says that the manifestation of the Spirit is given to each member of the church. The original King James Version declares that it is given to every man. That means every member of the church should have at least one of the nine gifts of the Spirit active and operational within their life. Everyone is designed to flow in at least one of the gifts of the Spirit. As a Spirit-filled believer, this is your normal!

The manner that these gifts manifest and flow within a church will vary from church to church. At our church, **High Praise Panama City**, an opportunity is made for the flow of the Holy Spirit during praise and worship. We also have post-service ministry teams available to minister at the end of services where prophetic words can be given. In general, we maintain a sensitivity to what the Holy Spirit desires to do within a service. Every service is different, and we allow Him to dictate and direct the flow that He desires.

Unfortunately, many local churches have a predetermined schedule for the service, and there can be no deviation. There is a certain time that everything is to happen. The flow of the Holy Spirit is not considered in the scheduling. Should anyone sense the flow moving in a direction contrary to the schedule, it is usually ignored and discarded. I am not throwing stones at churches that function in this manner. However, I am shining the light that the exclusion of the Holy Spirit forfeits His power and anointing from flowing within a service.

Continue in the Spirit

O foolish Galatians! Who has bewitched you that you should not obey the truth, before whose eyes Jesus Christ was clearly portrayed among you as crucified? This only I want to learn from you: Did you receive the Spirit by the works of the law, or by the hearing of faith?

Are you so foolish? Having begun in the Spirit, are you now being made perfect by the flesh? Have you suffered so many things in vain—if indeed it was in vain? Therefore He who supplies the Spirit to you and works miracles among you, does He do it by the works of the law, or by the hearing of faith? (Galatians 3:1-5).

Paul admonished the Galatians to continue in the Spirit; he said that if you begin in the Spirit, then continue in the Spirit. Leaning on fleshly means and mechanisms will not cause the church to become what Jesus desires. He sent the Holy Spirit because He wanted a flow in the church.

God designed us to flow; He designed the church to flow. We are incomplete without the flow of the Holy Spirit. Regardless of how large a church becomes, the moment they forsake the flow of the Holy Spirit, they start down the road of stagnation. Regardless of how "hip" the music and worship may be, if they forsake the flow of the Holy Spirit, it ends up being nothing more than a musical performance. The church is not a performing organization; it is a living organism. Ministry is designed to flow through us rather than entertainment performed by us.

There is a flow of the Holy Spirit that we are to release. Allow the rivers of living water to flow through you. You will be blessed and so will others when iFlow!

CHAPTER 8

iChange

IT IS IMPORTANT FOR US TO UNDERSTAND THAT WHILE THE FLESH RESISTS CHANGE, GROWTH REQUIRES IT.

> The Lord is not slack concerning His promise, as some count slackness, but is longsuffering toward us, not willing that any should perish but that all should come to repentance (2 Peter 3:9).

There is not a lot said about repentance today. Some even say that repentance is not necessary. Some see "repentance" as a bad word. They perceive it as a word that condemns others; however, "repentance" is a Bible word. It is a word that needs to be heard by both the church and the unchurched.

In the first message of Jesus preaching that we have recorded, He said, "Repent, for the kingdom of God is at hand" (Matthew 4:17). Well, if this was the first message Jesus preached, it must be important.

To fully understand repentance, we must define what it means. Repentance is derived from the Greek words *metanoia* or *metanoeo.* There are three different aspects within the definition that are all applicable and work together to produce the fruit of repentance within one's life. Repentance is not one dimensional, but rather multi-dimensional.

First, repentance means to change your mind. I would emphasize the word "change." At the heart of repentance is real change. To repent means that there has been a change in the way that you think about God, righteousness, yourself, and sin. True heart repentance will cause someone to turn from a lifestyle of sin. Repentance will cause someone to accept that Jesus has made them righteous through His blood. Change is a major part of repentance.

Secondly, repentance means compunction. It means to feel remorse, sorrow, or regret. I have found that those who are not sorrowful for their sin, never change their ways. If you can sin and not feel any remorse, there is an indication of a conscience that has been seared. The Bible also calls it "being past feeling" (Ephesians 4:19). This is what I call the **danger zone.** Our hearts should be tender toward the Holy Spirit and sense a pricking when we have missed the mark. I am not talking about condemnation, but rather a conviction that brings about repentance which should be present in the life of every believer.

The **third** aspect of repentance is to turn and walk in a different direction. This is the **action** part of repentance. True repentance will be exhibited through one's behavior.

You cannot truly repent of a sinful lifestyle and then continue to live in the same manner. You may have felt regret for your sin, but true repentance doesn't stop at a sense of regret or sorrow. Repentance will encompass an exhibited modification in one's behavior that is motivated and empowered by the grace of God.

You Need to Change

"Change" is not a word that we love to hear. For anyone who has been married for any length of time, I am sure they have heard their spouse say, "You need to change!" If we hear our spouse say that, we don't jump for joy and exclaim, "Thank you, Honey, for pointing that out to me. You are right; I do need to change. And because I love you so much, I am changing." That is not the usual discourse that takes place.

If we hear the word "change" from our mate, we typically will take a defensive posture. That's the way the flesh will react because it feels that it is being assaulted. From there, the response will be, "I need to change? I don't think so! Have you looked in the mirror lately?" The gloves come off all because we heard the word "CHANGE"!

Understand this: **spiritual growth begins the moment you embrace change.** The sooner you embrace change, the sooner you will begin the growth process. In the natural, when things grow, they change; however, as human beings, we can refuse to grow by refusing to change. To grow in grace, you must embrace change. You must embrace a lifestyle of repentance and change. As you do, you will grow.

Think about this: the first foundational doctrine of Christ is basically that you must change—repentance from dead works (Hebrews 6). This is what gets the wheels of salvation rolling in your life. That means that you stop doing the dead works that you did previously. You leave the sinful lifestyle you were embracing. Period. There is no going back; you have chosen to change!

Jesus and John the Baptist Preached Repentance

It's interesting to note that the command to repent and the message of repentance was preached repeatedly in the New Testament. John the Baptist preached one message the entire time he walked the earth: repent and be baptized. He preached a basic message of "turn or burn." John confronted the political and religious systems of the day and called for repentance. That is the only message John preached during his ministry. There are no recorded miracles that John performed. Yet, Jesus said that John was the greatest prophet to ever live upon the earth. Think about that.

The first recorded message that we observe Jesus preaching was "Repent, for the kingdom of heaven is at hand" (Matthew 4:17). Jesus took up where John the Baptist ended. He echoed what John had preached. Jesus also rebuked people who would not repent.

> "Then He began to rebuke the cities in which most of His mighty works had been done, because they did not repent" (Matthew 11:20).

Jesus took repentance seriously. The word "rebuke" means to defame, rail at, chide, and revile. This is what Jesus did to the cities who refused to change. Wow! Could it be that when we refuse to repent and embrace change that we position ourselves for rebuke rather than blessing? I believe it is much better to repent and change so we can position ourselves to receive blessing.

Peter and Paul Preached Repentance

Peter, on the day of Pentecost, in his first message said, "Repent!" (Acts 2:38). Obviously, it is of great importance if Peter declared it within the first message he preached after being filled with the Holy Spirit. He stated that the prerequisite for salvation and receiving the infilling of the Holy Spirit was repentance. If it was a requirement for the early church, then it is still a requirement today.

Almost every time Peter preached he said, "Repent!" In Peter's first message (Acts 2:38), second message (Acts 3:19), and then his third message (Acts 8:22) he used the word "repent." Well, where do you think Peter learned the importance of preaching repentance? Could it possibly be that he was following the example set for him through the ministry of Jesus? Could it be that he was echoing the same thing that Jesus preached? I believe so!

> "Truly, these times of ignorance God overlooked,
> but now commands all men everywhere to repent"
> (Acts 17:30).

When the apostle Paul comes on the scene, he begins to say the same thing; he begins to preach the importance of repentance and change. He says that God is now requiring a change in areas that were overlooked. Why would he say that? It is because **the grace of God and the Holy Spirit have now come to empower us to change.** Paul preached that we need the workings of repentance within our lives.

Grace to Change

While most theologians will attribute to Paul as being the messenger and expounder of the grace of God, it must be understood that grace without repentance is no longer grace. The word "grace" is defined in *Strong's Exhaustive Concordance* as "the divine influence upon the heart that is reflected in the life (or living)." A message of grace that ignores the necessity of repentance and change is not the message of grace that Paul preached.

Paul continually taught that believers should not be conformed to this world, but be transformed by the renewing of their minds. Bottom line—CHANGE! The word "transformed" is translated from the Greek word *metamorpho*. This is where we derive our English word "metamorphosis." It is the process that a caterpillar goes through to become a butterfly. There is great CHANGE that a caterpillar goes through to become a butterfly. On the other side of this metamorphic change, there is no resemblance between the caterpillar and butterfly.

Paul did not teach or preach that grace negated the importance of spiritual change within our lives. The new birth itself is a demonstrative change that takes place in our spirit man. It is then to be followed by change on the outside of man. Paul said that "old things have passed away, behold, all things have become new." That sounds like change to me!

Believers Should Repent

Another place we see the principle of repentance and change is in the book of Revelation. In chapters two and three of the book of Revelation, there are seven letters written to seven different churches. In five of the seven letters, Jesus tells them to "repent." He tells them the consequence if they don't repent and the blessing if they do.

Understand that these letters written to the churches are written to people who are saved. They are blood-washed, born-again Christians. Most likely they are all filled with the Holy Spirit. Yet, Jesus tells them to repent. That tells me this: repentance is not a "one and done" proposition. It is an ongoing principle that is to be activated and practiced within the lives of believers. Jesus said that even though you are saved, you must change!

We see that repentance is a kingdom message; change is a kingdom initiative. Everything God desires to do within our lives revolves around change beginning on the inside of us and then manifesting externally. Salvation is not to be viewed as a fire insurance policy merely to keep us from going to hell. This perspective cheapens and understates what Jesus did at the cross and the work of grace within our lives. His grace gives us power to change.

Jesus came to empower change within our lives. I heard a preacher say this, "God loves you so much that He will not allow you to remain the way you are." Along with the sense of belonging to the kingdom of God that we possess, there must also come the realization that God desires us to change. It is our responsibility to embrace the change that the Father desires to bring forth within our lives.

Resisting Change vs. Embracing Growth

When someone tells us to change, we usually begin to think that they have no business telling us such a thing. Someone saying that we need to change is viewed as an assault on our personage; it is seen as something meant to harm us. However, we must begin to view change as something that is good and helpful. It is something that will help propel us forward into destiny and purpose if we will only embrace it.

Human fleshly nature seems always to resist change. We are creatures of habit and don't want anyone to "rock the boat." We want everything to remain the way that it is. We have regular routines that have been developed and how dare anyone upset the norm. We have daily routines that we follow that if changed can cause us to react negatively.

It is important for us to understand that while the flesh resists change, growth requires it. The only things that are not growing are the things that reject change. Living organisms change in the growth process. While the basic structure of things may not change, growth will cause a change in its appearance and general character. For us to grow spiritually, we must embrace change. God will not force anyone to change; but, a lifestyle of repentance will require it.

This is the bottom line: **refusing change is refusing to grow.** Our personal growth is stunted the moment we say "no" to change. We stop dead in our tracks when we reject the change that God desires to bring into our lives.

God Uses Others to Help Us Change

I've heard people say, "I will change if God wants me to, but I'm not going to change because someone else said I need to." These people fail to realize that God uses others in our lives to help foster the change He desires to produce. God will use pastors, spiritual leaders, our spouses, and friends to speak the right word in due season. The angel of the Lord doesn't show up at the foot of our bed in the middle of the night and say, "You need to change." God uses others in the body of Christ and within our family.

> Brethren, if a man is overtaken in any trespass, you who are spiritual restore such a one in a spirit of gentleness, considering yourself lest you also be tempted (Galatians 6:1).

Paul is declaring in this passage of Scripture that when there is someone who needs to change, let others within the church help him. He didn't say to pray that they would receive angelic visitations or fresh revelations. He said that others in the church are to function as agents of restoration and change.

Spiritual growth begins the moment that repentance is activated. The work of repentance within our lives will cause us to put aside the things of the flesh and embrace the work of the Spirit. It will cause us to reject the old way and receive the newness of the Spirit. Repentance will act as a springboard that thrusts us into the fulfillment of God's purpose and plan for our lives.

> If we say that we have no sin, we deceive ourselves, and the truth is not in us. If we confess our sins, He is faithful and just to forgive us our sins and to cleanse us from all unrighteousness (1 John 1:8-9).

This is a wonderful passage of Scripture that I have known my entire life. I was blessed and privileged to be brought up in a Christian home and went to church regularly (at least once a week). I also attended a Christian school throughout my elementary years and had a Bible class where we memorized Scripture. First John 1:9 was one of the first Scriptures I learned.

There has been much debate in recent years as to whom this particular verse of Scripture was written. Also, there has been debate concerning how it should be applied in the life of the believer. Some have gone so far as to say that it is not applicable at all in the life of a Christian. However, I think that sometimes we fail to see the forest for the trees.

I believe there is an overarching biblical principle found within this passage of Scripture. That principle is that we should live a lifestyle of repentance and change. In doing so, we embrace the fullness of God's grace.

Confessing the Need for Change

If we can for just a moment talk about "sin." The word "sin" literally means to miss the mark or be mistaken. It means to fall short. I believe that we would all agree that there are areas where we miss the mark, are mistaken, or fall short of God's standard. These are areas where we must place a demand on the grace of God and the work of the Holy Spirit to empower us to overcome. John is talking about areas where we need to change.

With that in mind, let's again examine this Scripture passage, and I will add my commentary:

> If we confess our sins [we acknowledge our need to change], He is faithful and just to forgive us our sins [empower us to change and live differently] and to cleanse us from all unrighteousness [we will be empowered to live differently] (1 John 1:9).

My commentary inserted is meant only to bring an understanding of a biblical principle that is contained in this passage. Understand this: a person will not change in an area that they believe themselves to be right or justified. People who live a lifestyle of justifying everything they do will not embrace repentance and change. The most difficult people to deal with are those who justify themselves. They are usually hard-headed and stubborn because they have "deceived" themselves.

Deception and Self-Justification

This is what John is speaking of in these verses when he says, "We deceive ourselves." Denying the existence of fault and the need for change is self-deception. Justifying sin and saying we don't need to change is deception in manifestation. However, John also declared that living a lifestyle of repentance, where we embrace change within our lives, will empower the grace of God to be active. We will be cleansed (the area of fault removed) from all unrighteousness.

We can see this principle at work in the life of King Saul and David. Samuel confronted Saul for his disobedience to the word of the Lord. Saul, in turn, justified himself and blamed the people. The end result of Saul's prideful self-justification was the loss of the kingdom of Israel.

David, on the other hand, repented of his sin with Bathsheba and of having Uriah killed when confronted by the prophet Nathan. He said, "I am the man." David admitted his fault and his need for change. David was quick to repent for his sin. He acknowledged his wrongdoing and need for change.

God forgave David, but removed the Kingdom from Saul. Why was the result for David different than Saul? It was because David confessed his sin, while Saul was consumed with denial and self-justification. If we are quick to say, "I need to change," God will forgive and empower us to overcome. If we say that "we have no sin" (no need to change), we become those who are resistant to the truth.

Today, I encourage you to embrace change; embrace a lifestyle of repentance. It will make a difference in your life. It will set you on the road of life and will take you off the road to destruction. New joy will abound as you live your life at a higher level that He has for you. This happens when you say, "iChange."

CHAPTER 9

iGive

GIVING IS THE PRINCIPLE THAT GOD ESTABLISHED TO RELEASE HIS BLESSING WITHIN THE EARTH.

"Give, and it will be given to you: good measure, pressed down, shaken together, and running over will be put into your bosom. For with the same measure that you use, it will be measured back to you" (Luke 6:38).

These words of Jesus are of great importance within the lives of believers. Giving is a biblical principle that is clearly articulated throughout the Bible. It is a principle of the kingdom of God that all Christians must embrace to see the fullness of God's blessing manifested within their lives.

As I stated previously, I grew up in a Christian home. My father and mother were givers; it was their lifestyle. They lived to give and be a blessing to others. They taught both my brother and me to live in the same manner.

I can fondly remember my parents teaching us to tithe on our allowance. That meant we were to give ten percent of what we were given when the offering was received at church. During my childhood, that was a grand total of a nickel since our allowance was just 50 cents. My parents stressed to me that it was not the amount, but the principle. They taught me to be faithful in the little so that God would release more into my life.

The reality is that giving is a command. Jesus never suggested that we give; rather He commanded it. Giving is to become a lifestyle within the life of the believer. Jesus even gave us some incentive; He said if we give, it would be given back to us in an increased manner. Jesus declared that blessing would overtake those who are faithful to give to the Lord.

So, where does giving begin? Giving begins with the tithe which is ten percent of all your increase.

> "For I am the LORD, I do not change; Therefore you are not consumed, O sons of Jacob. Yet from the days of your fathers You have gone away from My ordinances And have not kept them. Return to Me, and I will return to you," Says the LORD of hosts. "But you said, 'In what way shall we return?' Will a man rob God? Yet you have robbed Me! But you say, 'In what way have we robbed You?' In tithes and offerings. You are cursed with a curse, For you have robbed Me, Even this whole nation. Bring all the tithes into the storehouse, That there may be food in My

house, And try Me now in this," Says the LORD of hosts, "If I will not open for you the windows of heaven And pour out for you such blessing That there will not be room enough to receive it. And I will rebuke the devourer for your sakes, So that he will not destroy the fruit of your ground, Nor shall the vine fail to bear fruit for you in the field," Says the LORD of hosts; And all nations will call you blessed, For you will be a delightful land," Says the LORD of hosts (Malachi 3:6-12).

Notice that God declares to His people that He will bless them if they are faithful to bring the tithe (10 percent) to the house of the Lord. He declares that blessing will be multiplied in their lives as the result of giving.

Tithing—A Kingdom Principle

There are some who have attempted to negate the necessity of the tithe by saying that it was only for those under the Law of Moses. However, a complete study of Scripture will reveal that tithing is a kingdom principle that originated before the Law of Moses was even given. I would also like to bring your attention to the verse of Scripture located immediately before this discourse on tithing where God says, "I am the Lord, I do not change." In other words, God is letting us know that the He is not changing His principle and precept that He initiated concerning the tithe.

The first mention of the tithe begins with Abraham giving a tithe to Melchizedek which was hundreds of years before the Law was given. We also see Jesus teaching on the importance of the tithe when He said that you ought to tithe (Matthew 23:23). Jesus, while ministering during a time when the Law was still in force, taught prophetically concerning New Testament truths. He revealed things to come in the New Covenant while walking on the earth during the Old Covenant. Jesus revealed the truth that tithing ought to be done.

The writer of Hebrews also spoke of tithing when He said, "Here men that die receive tithes, but there He receives them" (Hebrews 7:8). He indicated that while men here on earth receive the tithe, Jesus receives it since He is a priest after the order of Melchizedek. As Abraham brought the tithe to Melchizedek, we continue the same pattern as the seed of Abraham, and Jesus receives it.

Five-Fold Blessing of the Tithe

There is a **five-fold blessing** that we see specifically mentioned concerning those who tithe and give offerings. The **first** blessing is that of spiritual food. There will be spiritual food for those who are faithful with their tithe and offering. As we give of the natural things that God has given us, He will be faithful to give us spiritual sustenance.

I have found that people who are not faithful in their giving are usually the ones who will be heard saying, "I'm not being fed." Contrariwise, those who are faithful with their tithe and offerings are generally the ones who are declaring how much they are receiving and growing spiritually. The interesting thing is that they are all hearing the same thing. However, those who give are fed, while those who fail to give appear to experience famine. The first blessing that God releases to the giver is spiritual food.

The **second** blessing of the tither is an open heaven with a blessing poured out. There is no such thing as a closed heaven in the life of the giver. Givers will live under an open heaven and blessing will be poured out in an abundant measure.

God declares that the tither will experience blessing in a manner where it cannot be contained. This sounds very similar to what Jesus said about giving. He said that as we give, it would be given back to us until it is "running over" (Luke 6:38) which means there's no room to receive it. That's El-Shaddai—the God who is more than enough—being revealed in your life! Hallelujah!

The **third** blessing of the tither is that the devourer is rebuked by the Lord of Hosts. Many believers don't realize that giving is a weapon of spiritual warfare. Tithing will empower the Lord to fight on your behalf. He will arise as a man of war (Exodus 20:3), and the enemy will be scattered as you give.

It's interesting to note that at the end of the statement declaring the devourer will be rebuked, Scripture specifically emphasizes that the Lord of Hosts is speaking. *Lord of Hosts* literally means the Lord of armies and warriors. God is declaring that He will fight on our behalf with the armies of heaven when we are faithful with our tithe and offering. The enemies of lack, poverty, and insufficiency will be rebuked and sent running.

I personally believe that giving is not merely a weapon of warfare against our financial enemies, but also any spiritual enemy that would try to raise its head. **Giving acts as a divine canopy of protection from the onslaught of the devil.** God will arise on behalf of those who are faithful with their tithe and offering.

The **fourth** blessing of the tither is fruitfulness. Since Israel was primarily an agricultural nation, this promise dealt specifically with their physical crops that were being grown and harvested. The contemporary application within our lives is fruitfulness and promotion in the arena of job and career. Another way of saying this is that whatever you put your hand to do will prosper.

God promises to bless you in the pursuit of a good job and career. He will bless your business and all with which you involve yourself. God will not only provide a good job for you, but He will also promote you where you are. He declared to His covenant people that they would be the head and not the tail (Deuteronomy 28:13). That means God will enable you to be promoted and exalted in the workplace. Hallelujah!

The **fifth** blessing of the tither is an undeniable and recognizable manifested blessing. God said that all nations (peoples) will call you blessed. In other words, people will look at the tither and declare, "They are surely blessed." Well, the only way that someone is going to look at you and say you are blessed is if there is an evident blessing in your life. No one looks at the individual on Skid Row and says, "Wow, they sure are blessed."

God declares that those who are givers will experience manifested blessing within their lives. He says that it will be apparent. The blessing will be so abundant that others who don't know the Lord will comment on how much blessing is manifesting in their lives. This is the manner in which God will bless the giver—the one who tithes and gives offerings.

The First-Fruits of All Your Increase

Giving is the doorway to increase; it unlocks things that were previously unattainable. Unexplainable things happen within the lives of givers. I've seen it repeatedly occur throughout my life. God supernaturally releases blessing and wealth into the hands of those who honor the Lord with their first-fruits.

> Honor the LORD with your possessions, And with the firstfruits of all your increase; So your barns will be filled with plenty, And your vats will overflow with new wine (Proverbs 3:9-10).

Notice what is said in this passage of Scripture: honor the Lord with the FIRST-FRUITS of all your increase. The first-fruits are the first part; we should never give to the Lord what we have left over. We should always give to Him FIRST. It is imperative that the Lord be honored with the first part which is the tithe.

I've heard people say, "I can't afford to tithe." My response is, "You can't afford not to tithe." Stealing from the Lord is not the path to prosperity. Withholding from the Lord will not release His blessing; it will actually empower the curse within one's life.

God said that those who refuse to tithe are robbing from God. In other words, holding back the first ten percent of your increase is stealing from the Lord. In the world today, if you are caught with stolen goods, you go to jail. Could it be that many are spiritually imprisoning themselves because of their failure to live as givers? Could it be that many forfeit the manifested blessing of the Lord because they are holding on to what belongs to Him? Think about it!

God promises that those who honor the Lord with their first-fruits will experience their barns filled with plenty. He continues by saying that their vats will "overflow" with new wine. Once again, we see the concept of overflow being articulated. Malachi said it. Jesus said it, and now Solomon said it. Wow!

Giving Releases Natural and Spiritual Blessing

We see in this passage of Scripture from Proverbs a reference to both natural and spiritual blessing. The best present-day application for the promise of plenty is that your bank account and wallet will have more than enough; you will not lack for anything financially. Abundance will be your close friend and companion. Poverty, lack, and insufficiency will be unable to visit your household!

The spiritual blessing of this verse of Scripture is contained in the declaration that your "vats will overflow with new wine." New wine is a type of the Holy Spirit. The promise is that the work of the Holy Spirit within your life will overflow to the point that others are affected. The anointing will be released, and bondages will be broken and destroyed. The new wine (Holy Spirit) will not only affect you, but your family, relatives, and friends, too! This is the promise to all who are faithful with their tithes and offerings.

The Consequence of Stealing from God

In the Old Testament, a man by the name of Achan took what had been set apart and consecrated to the Lord. The very FIRST battle going into the Promised Land was the city of Jericho. The people were commanded not to touch or take anything in the city. The spoils were to be given to the Lord; it was to be the FIRST-fruits of victory.

Achan saw valuable things, took them, and hid it in his tent. As a result, the Israelites suffered a crushing defeat in the next battle at Ai. One man's sin caused the entire nation to suffer. Achan's sin was exposed. Then he, his entire family, and all his livestock were destroyed. What a horrible end!

Achan could have stolen things from other people and not have experienced the same end. However, the moment he touched what God said belonged to Him, Achan sealed his fate. The moment Achan robbed from God by withholding the FIRST-fruits, he signed his own death warrant.

119

I'm not saying that anyone is going to die because of their failure to give. However, things within your life may end abruptly. Financial difficulty may onset when anyone decides to take what belongs to the Lord. On the other hand, giving will release abundant blessing. Which would you prefer? I prefer the blessing! So iGive!

Jehovah-Jireh—My Provider

When we give, we acknowledge that God is our provider. Giving is the declaration of our trust in the Lord for provision and sustenance. It is the action part of our faith that God is Jehovah-Jireh—the One who sees and provides.

Giving is the principle that God has established to release His blessing within the earth. When we acknowledge Him as provider through our giving, He is released to be our Provider. He desires to bless us, but we must allow Him to do so, and this is done through giving.

In many churches today, tithing and giving offerings are no longer taught. It is said that people may become offended if anything is said concerning money. Unfortunately, people end up perishing financially for the lack of knowledge. Failure to preach the truth for fear that someone may be offended is compromise with a capital "C"! Pastors who do this should either change quickly or hand over their church to someone who will preach the truth.

Jesus taught kingdom principles concerning giving. Abraham exhibited giving. Paul wrote on giving in numerous epistles. David demonstrated the lifestyle of a giver when he said, "I will not give to God that which costs me nothing" (2 Samuel 24:24). The principle of giving is scattered throughout the Bible from Genesis chapter one through the ending chapter of the book of Revelation. If this truth is so prolific in the Bible, we should preach it, teach it, and practice it. iGive should be something we do with joy and expectation!

Make a decision from this day forward to live as a giver, rather than a taker. Commit to honoring the Lord with the first-fruits of all that you receive. You will then be able to say, "My barns are filled with plenty because iGive. Blessing abounds in my life because iGive."

CHAPTER 10

> OFFENSE AND UNFORGIVENESS ARE THE THINGS THAT OPEN THE DOOR TO HELL AND ALL ITS GARBAGE.

Be sober, be vigilant; because your adversary the devil walks about like a roaring lion, seeking whom he may devour. Resist him, steadfast in the faith, knowing that the same sufferings are experienced by your brotherhood in the world (1 Peter 5:8-9).

In this chapter, I want to discuss the most dangerous enemies of the believer. They destroy God-ordained relationships. They cause people to disconnect from the local church, its leaders, and sometimes the entire body of Christ. These enemies wreck the lives of Christians and spiritually paralyze them from fulfilling destiny and purpose. They will cause believers never to have a sense of belonging because they produce a tinted and tainted view of others within the Church. The enemies I am speaking of are offense, unforgiveness, and bitterness.

I have personally seen more lives and relationships destroyed through these things than through adultery, pornography, alcoholism, or drug addiction. I've seen more people shipwrecked as the result of these spiritual cancers than anything else in my almost four decades of ministry. These are the things that the devil will use to devour unknowing Christians. He seeks entrance into the lives of believers through the doorway of offense, unforgiveness, and bitterness.

Believers can overcome these enemies if we are aware of them, how they work, the strategies that the devil uses to unleash them, and most importantly the power of our weaponry to combat them. In this chapter, I want to do more than merely illuminate these things, but also give you a spiritual strategy to combat and overcome them in Jesus' name.

Shut the Door and Keep the Devil Out

Peter said that our adversary goes about "seeking whom he may devour." One important thing to realize is that the enemy cannot devour everyone. He must look for someone who has an open door for him to enter. The devil doesn't have the authority to invade the life of a believer without an avenue of access.

We have doors on the homes where we live which provide entrance and exit for those who live there. They are also instrumental in keeping out people and creatures that don't belong inside. There are spiritual doors in your life that are meant to be closed to keep out the devil and open to receive from the Spirit of the Lord. The enemy has no access unless we open the door for him. We must keep the door slammed in the face of the enemy.

If we choose to take an offense and walk in unforgiveness, we open the door for the enemy to gain entrance. Offense and unforgiveness are the things that open the door to hell and all its garbage. They bring deception and delusion, and they produce slander and lying. These are just some of the things that enter someone's life when unforgiveness takes root.

It's a Trap

"A brother offended is harder to be won than a strong city: and their contentions are like the bars of a castle" (Proverbs 18:19).

Offense will bring bondage and imprisonment into the lives of those who embrace it. Living as someone who is offended will only hurt you—the person who is upset, mad, and angry. However, it has lasting consequences that affect many.

In the New Testament, the Greek word that is translated "offense" is *skandalon* which means a trap or snare. Offense and unforgiveness are the snares that satan uses to trap believers. He is then able to devour them. Those who are easily offended become the devil's next meal.

We must understand that it is critical in the life of a believer to guard against these things. Why? It is because you will never be able to say "iBelong" while you walk in offense and unforgiveness. It will sabotage any sense of belonging within a believer's life.

This particular topic is worthy of an entire book; however, I will condense things significantly for the purposes of this writing. There are some great books already written on these topics—among them, *The Bait of Satan* by John Bevere (Charisma House).

"Looking carefully lest anyone fall short of the grace of God; lest any root of bitterness springing up cause trouble, and by this many become defiled" (Hebrews 12:15).

The progression of offense, unforgiveness, and bitterness is a trap into which many believers fall. What starts as an offense turns into unforgiveness. As that is rehearsed repeatedly, it becomes a root of bitterness. The end result is broken relationships; it causes believers to separate from who and where they belong. Long-standing relationships end up on the rocks because of these enemies.

Once someone becomes offended, unless that offense is addressed, it will turn into unforgiveness. If someone continues to hold on to the unforgiveness, it will then turn into a root of bitterness. These roots within a believer's life are destructive. Many people in the church are harmed when bitterness springs up in someone's life.

I have witnessed people hang on to an offense and get bitter. Eventually, their vision becomes skewed. It doesn't matter how much people reach out to them in love; there is always something wrong with everyone else. They feel they don't belong because they are blinded by their own bitterness. Those who live in this manner ultimately contaminate others in the church. They become poison in the body of Christ and hurt many believers.

Skewed Perspective

When people walk in unforgiveness, their perspective becomes twisted. This type of skewed perspective causes people to see things incorrect and distorted. When people are hurt and operate dysfunctionally, they can become delusional to the point that reality is no longer relative—truth is only what they perceive regardless of facts. Things get warped and augmented. This can sometimes be the result of a Leviathan spirit at work.

Ultimately, relationships are broken because these unforgiving people accuse others of things that never happened. They project their own behavior onto those with whom they are offended. They sabotage relationships and then blame the innocent for doing it. Rather than seeking resolution and reconciliation, they long for retribution and vindication for things that never happened or that they brought upon themselves.

Those who operate in this manner need much prayer and deliverance. If you find yourself operating in this manner, then STOP! The first step to freedom is to acknowledge the problem, confess it, and cry out to God for help. He will be faithful to deliver those who call on His name.

We must realize that the devil is the one who causes people to have a skewed perspective. Another word for this is "deception" which causes God-ordained relationships to be destroyed. We must be aware that this is one of satan's schemes.

Absalom's Offense

When you read the account of Absalom, you will see the event which caused him to spiral down the rabbit hole. His sister, Tamar, was raped by his half-brother, Amnon (2 Samuel 13). Afterward, Amnon hated Tamar, sent her away, and bolted the door behind her. This was an act of extreme hatred and rejection.

Tamar told Absalom what happened. He, in turn, told his sister to keep it to herself and not to take it to heart. She remained in his house, but desolate. Then we read what happened in Absalom's life.

"And Absalom spoke to his brother Amnon neither good nor bad. For Absalom hated Amnon, because he had forced his sister Tamar" (2 Samuel 13:22).

Absalom told his sister not to take to heart what happened to her (don't be offended). However, he took an offense, walked in unforgiveness, and became bitter. This was the process that sent Absalom down the road of destruction.

Jesus said that if your brother offends you, go to him. Absalom refused to speak to his brother at all. Jesus said to love your enemy. Absalom hated his brother which cultivated a root of bitterness in his heart. He fertilized the seeds of offense by refusing to talk to Amnon. His hatred grew as he walked in unforgiveness. Ultimately, the root of bitterness was planted so deep within Absalom's life that two years later he murdered Amnon.

Time Makes It Worse

There was a two-year time lapse between the time Tamar was raped and the murder of Absalom's brother. However, he began his plot on the day that his sister was raped by Amnon.

"... for only Amnon is dead. For by the command of Absalom this has been determined from the day that he forced his sister Tamar" (2 Samuel 13:32).

Absalom had already planned and plotted the murder of Amnon from day one. For two years, he meditated on it. For two years, he planned it. For two years, he fantasized about Amnon's blood being spilled. Finally, at the right moment, his plan was hatched.

For two years, Absalom could have been working on removing the offense. For two years, he could have been declaring forgiveness. For two years, he could have been having a dialogue with his brother. However, he chose to embrace the vicious cycle of offense, unforgiveness, and bitterness. He opened the door for the enemy, and the devil obliged him.

Forfeited Destiny and Double the Sinner

This story is tragic. Absalom was a prince in the Kingdom in line for the throne. However, he forfeited his purpose and destiny because he took an offense. Everything that God destined him to become in the kingdom of Israel was flushed down the toilet. It was not because of something done to him, but because he took the offense of another—the offense of his sister.

I can understand Absalom's anger. I can understand the feelings of rage that he probably experienced. However, that doesn't make anything he did right. Someone may have a natural justification for being angry, but it will never justify unforgiveness and bitterness. That is the road to disaster.

Later in Absalom's life, he became twice the sinner. While his half-brother had raped his sister, he raped all of his father's concubines in plain view of the nation.

"So they pitched a tent for Absalom on the top of the house, and Absalom went in to his father's concubines in the sight of all Israel" (2 Samuel 16:22).

The very thing that Absalom abhorred Amnon for doing, raping a family member, he did to a greater degree in front of the nation. He did this to spite his father and position himself as the leader. His motivation for doing this was power and influence. He desired to show the nation that he was the one in charge and that he had taken the place of his father, David. This was despicable.

Forgive and Refrain from Reproducing

Jesus commanded us to forgive. Then on the heels of that, He said whoever sins you retain, they are retained and whoever sins you forgive, they are forgiven (John 20:23). Jesus wasn't giving His disciples the power to forgive people of their sins; rather, He was articulating a spiritual principle at work. That principle is when you choose to forgive, that sin is released from you. That sin is disempowered from being reproduced through you. However, when you choose to walk in unforgiveness, you retain that sin and then reproduce it in your own life. The sin you retain is the open door for the enemy to build a stronghold within your life. This is what happened to Absalom.

Ultimately, Absalom is destroyed. His father wept at the news of his death. Absalom's demise was self-inflicted; he brought it upon himself through unforgiveness. Many believe Absalom's demise was because he led a rebellion. However, the rebellion was merely a manifestation of the root of bitterness. His sin didn't start as a rebellion; it began as an offense taken.

The reason I am taking time to share this story is to reveal how this dangerous progression of destruction operates. Paul said, "We are not ignorant of [the devil's] devices" (2 Corinthians 2:11). **We need to understand exactly how the enemy takes advantage of believers and traps them through offense and unforgiveness.** This will help prevent us from being satan's next meal. He can't devour me because I am aware of his devices.

Let It Go

Many people come into local churches with baggage. They feel they have been mistreated and abused. They have a list of the people who have done them wrong and can recite every wrong that they have ever experienced. Unfortunately, if they don't LET IT GO, they will never experience a sense of belonging. They will see the world through the pain they experienced yesterday.

Most of the time, when someone walks in unforgiveness, they will distance themselves from the offending party. They will give them the "cold shoulder" which is a fleshly human response. It is carried out when one feels that they have been harmed in some way or another. There are also people who do this in an attempt to punish the individual whom they feel hurt them. All of this is fleshly and carnal; it is not the love of God in action.

As long as a person hangs on to yesterday's offense, they will imprison themselves. They will be chained to the events of the past and paralyzed from moving forward into purpose and destiny. In actuality, satan can sit back and watch as they incarcerate themselves through offense, unforgiveness, and bitterness. The end result is self-inflicted destruction. My friend, it's not worth it! Let it go!

The Poison You Shouldn't Drink

The amazing thing about unforgiveness is that people who choose to hold on to things believe they are exacting retribution on the offender. Get this: unforgiveness is like drinking poison expecting someone else to die. The reality is no one is harmed immediately by unforgiveness other than the offended person. They are the ones that reap the negative consequences. They are the ones that drink the poison. The greatest consequences of this behavior are the loss of relationship and the sense of not belonging.

If someone put poison in front of you and told you to drink it, you would not do it. The reason for this is because you want to remain alive. However, many believers are drinking the poison that satan places in front of them. It's in a bottle labeled offense, unforgiveness, and bitterness. It's in a bottle that has a cap labeled revenge and retribution. It promises to quench your thirst for justice and vindication. However, the person that you despise will not be harmed when you drink it; they will only attend your funeral. My friend, don't drink it!

There are some practical spiritual principles that we can enact to prevent this demonic and fleshly progression. If we do these things, we will avoid becoming trapped in the snare of the enemy. We will overcome and triumph in the name of Jesus.

Walk in Love

The **first principle** to overcome offense is to **walk in love**. Many people don't realize that walking in love is one of the greatest defenses we possess. The Bible says that love keeps no record of wrong (1 Corinthians 13:5). Love doesn't keep score. You can't walk in love and unforgiveness at the same time.

There is no room for bitterness when you are filled with the love of God. Walking in love will keep you from taking an offense from the start. It will guard your heart against the ploy of the enemy. It will combat hatred and resentment.

It is essential to understand that love is a verb; it's not a feeling. Love is not determined by how you feel. Instead, it is determined by what you do. Walking in the love of God is a decision of heart that we make. We can choose to love people even in the absence of feelings of fondness. It is a choice that we make. I encourage you to make that choice. Walk in love.

Choose to Forgive

Another principle to enact is simply to **choose forgiveness**. I was counseling someone years ago, and I told them they needed to forgive an individual. They replied, "Well, they didn't say they were sorry." It's important to realize that rendering forgiveness should not be predicated on a repentant heart from the offending party. Jesus said that we are to forgive with no exceptions. Regardless of an articulated apology, we choose to forgive.

Many years ago, a minister spoke some things falsely about me. The things he said prevented me from being employed by a ministry that was desiring me to be their music director. When I found out what he said, I was shocked and hurt. Soon that hurt turned to anger.

It just so happened that I had to drive by this minister's church regularly. Every time I would drive by their building, something would arise within me. Unfortunately, it was not the Spirit of the Lord. The reality was that I was offended, hurt, angry, and resentful. This was slowly turning to bitterness.

One day, as I was driving by his building, the Lord spoke to me. He told me, "Every time you drive by here, extend your hand and say, 'I forgive and release you.'" So, I started doing that. It was difficult at first. However, the more I did it, the easier it got. Several months later, I noticed that I drove by the building and didn't even realize it. I knew then that forgiveness had been realized.

The gnawing in my gut was no longer there; the feelings of resentment had disappeared. It was no longer something that haunted me. I had overcome offense, unforgiveness, and bitterness because I had chosen to forgive.

About six months later, I had lunch with this minister. During our meal, he apologized to me for what he had said. I expressed that I received his apology. The reality was that I had already forgiven him in months previous because I couldn't afford to wait for him to apologize. I couldn't afford to drink poison for six months. Think about it.

You Can't Escape Yourself

The reason it was so important for me to forgive is that if I had failed to overcome bitterness at that time, it would have followed me everywhere from that point on. You must understand that your issues will not change because you move geographically; they will follow you wherever you go. Distance and time away from the situation will not heal anything. Absalom didn't talk to his brother, Amnon, for two years. Time and absence didn't change or heal the situation; it only grew worse.

I have told people that a new house, new job, new car, new spouse, new location, or a new church will not change a bitter heart or bad attitude. The truth is that you take YOU wherever you go. You cannot escape yourself. None of us can. Any issue of offense, unforgiveness, or bitterness will follow you wherever you go unless you deal with it and choose to let it go.

Unrealistic Expectations

The **third principle** is to **never expect from others what you don't deliver yourself**. I have witnessed people getting upset because someone did something to them that they themselves were known to do. Expecting others to behave in a way that you don't is hypocritical.

One day I was walking in the mall with my wife and another friend of our family. As we walked, we passed by a person that was known by our friend. Neither one of them said anything to the other. After the person passed by, our friend looked at my wife and said indignantly, "Did you see that? She didn't even speak to me!" My wife boldly replied, "Well, you didn't talk to her either." That went over like a lead balloon.

Our friend was upset and offended that someone did not speak to them. However, they were guilty of the exact same thing. Their expectation for others was greater than what they had for themselves.

Jesus said to do unto others as you would have them do unto you. He didn't say to expect from others what you don't deliver yourself. Doing unto others what you desire yourself is love in action. Expecting from others what you don't deliver is selfish and narcissistic. People who live with unrealistic expectations will also live offended. They will live disappointed with everyone else. They will live upset with others for what they practice themselves.

We must learn to give grace to others. Give grace in the same manner that you desire. Refuse to live with unrealistic expectations of others.

Take the High Road

If there is strife or division between you and another person in the church, you must ask yourself this, "Do I want to be right or reconciled?" I will tell you that the flesh always wants to be declared right. The reason people will argue and bicker for prolonged periods of time is that one or both want vindication. They want to be declared right and the winner.

Understand this: just because you are right, doesn't make your actions right. You can be right, but be wrong at the same time. If you value being declared right more than being reconciled with your brother, then you are wrong. It is more important that our relationships are right and reconciled than being told we are right.

Jesus said, "Agree with your adversary quickly (Matthew 5:25)." He told us to refrain from getting into heated arguments and debates with people. He encouraged us to value the relationship more than being declared the rightful winner.

I have found that many times, in the middle of disagreements, you may be able to argue someone into a place of surrender where they finally say, "I was wrong."

However, their flag of surrender and admission doesn't necessarily mean that they believed it. They merely said it to bring the argument to an end. So, in the long run, this kind of behavior has no long-lasting fruit. It will usually only cause resentment in the person that is forced to surrender. Learn to take the high road. Value relationships more than being told you are right.

Family and Forgiveness

There is no such thing as a family without forgiveness. Likewise, there is no church body without forgiveness in operation. Family cannot succeed without the functioning of forgiveness. Jesus said that where two people gather together in His name, He is there in the midst of them (Matthew 18:20). I've concluded where two are gathered together in any situation there is an opportunity for offense.

My wife and I have been married for 38 years. I have lost count of the number of times that I have apologized to her; I'm sure she has done the same. Someone said, "Love is never having to say I'm sorry." That's a joke. The reality is that love is repeatedly saying you're sorry.

The majority of things for which I have apologized to my wife are things that I never did deliberately. However, I may have said something improperly to her. Her feelings were hurt, and I needed to say, "I'm sorry." Why? It is because I love her, and our relationship is more important than my pride.

I remember a time many years ago that we were getting ready to go to church on a Sunday morning. I was required to be there at a particular time since I was a staff member. We were running a little late that morning. My wife asked me, "How do I look?" I promptly and abruptly said, "Fine. Let's go!" What I actually communicated to her was, "I don't care what you look like; we are running late, so get in the car right now!"

She made sure that I knew that I hurt her feelings. After some discussion, I apologized for my abruptness. I could have attempted to justify my sharpness by saying, "You should be ready early if you want a polite response because I have things to do and places to be!" That would have only made things worse.

Anytime you attempt to justify offending someone, you only make things worse and drive a wedge in the relationship. It creates a greater challenge for the offended person to overcome. On top of the hurt they experience, they now have a larger mountain to climb to arrive at realized forgiveness.

The other side of this equation is that the person offended must choose to forgive regardless. Getting angry, upset, and resentful will only make you miserable. Learn to let it go and move on. Don't let hurtful things be the soundtrack of your life. Choose to be reconciled.

If we always value reconciliation more than anything else, peace will be the outcome. There are rare occasions when someone refuses to be reconciled which is the exception rather than the rule. Always seek reconciliation and resolution. It is the path to restored relationships.

The Balance of Forgiveness

It's important for us to understand the balance to forgiveness. Realize that forgiveness and restoration are two different things. When we forgive someone, we release them and choose to hold no ill will, negative judgment, or bitterness toward them. However, forgiveness does not always necessitate relational restoration with those who have unhealthy and harmful behavioral patterns that they will neither acknowledge or change. This is especially true when there are abusive and manipulative practices involved within the life of the offender.

In other words, I can forgive someone without reconnecting relationally with them if they are unwilling to change their behavior. If they are willing to acknowledge and change their behavior, then there is opportunity for the relationship to be mended. Forgiveness functions independently of restoration.

All of the aforementioned principles, when enacted, will cause the patterns of offense, unforgiveness, and bitterness to cease. It will bring the rejection cycle to an end. There will be a sense of belonging and acceptance that you will realize. You will not be the one on the outside looking in; you will know that you belong.

Make a decision today that you will refuse to allow the enemies of offense, unforgiveness, and bitterness to take root in your life. So, choose to forgive, release, and get over it! Then you will be able to say, "iForgive and iBelong!"

CHAPTER 11

iBelieve

PART 1

> TO BE A PART OF A LOCAL CHURCH BODY, IT IS IMPORTANT THAT EVERYONE HAS ELEMENTARY AND FOUNDATIONAL UNDERSTANDING OF BASIC BIBLE DOCTRINES.

Therefore, leaving the discussion of the elementary principles of Christ, let us go on to perfection, not laying again the foundation of repentance from dead works and of faith toward God, of the doctrine of baptisms, of laying on of hands, of resurrection of the dead, and of eternal judgment (Hebrews 6:1-2).

In this passage of Scripture, we see what is referred to as the Six Foundational Doctrines of Christ. We will briefly discuss these doctrines in this chapter and the next. These are essential things for believers to know and ascribe. While each doctrine is entitled to an entire dissertation that would be longer than this entire writing, we will summarize these for our purposes and only concentrate on the primary points.

I have purposefully broken up these foundational doctrines into two parts. The first four are primarily involved in what we do presently on earth and our ministries within the local church. The last two foundational doctrines are primarily related to what we believe concerning the coming of the Lord and eternity.

To be a part of a local church body, it is important that everyone has an elementary and foundational understanding of fundamental Bible doctrines. While churches, fellowships, and denominations may differ on some things, there are some fundamental truths that are held within the body of Christ at large. Every church will have its version of basic doctrines, but it is important that we know them if we are going to participate and function within that body of believers.

Paul told the church at Corinth that they were to all "speak the same thing." That meant they were not to be divided in what they believed. There were certain elementary foundations of the faith that they all were to agree upon and speak congruently.

Steadfast in Doctrine

The Bible declares that in the early Church "they continued steadfastly in the apostles' doctrine" (Acts 2:42). That means they were taught doctrines that they were to believe and adhere in order to anchor their faith. The only thing that possessed the power to do that was the infallible Word of God. This is what the apostles taught the early Church.

The early apostles did not teach from **Reader's Digest** or the latest article from **Psychology Today** magazine. I'm not saying these magazines are bad; they just don't belong where doctrine and sound teaching are to be propagated. We cannot substitute nice, heart-warming stories and psychological analysis for doctrinal foundations and biblical teaching.

Much of the Bible teaching that was received decades ago within the church is no longer taught and propagated in the contemporary church culture of today. Many have substituted entertainment in the pulpit for the impartation of sound doctrine and preaching of the Word of God. Unfortunately, in our attempt to reach the masses, we have lost much of our impact. I'm not saying this to be critical, rather to illuminate an issue that needs to be corrected. This also brings a realization of the need for instruction in basic biblical foundations.

Biblical Literacy

Below is an excerpt from an article published by *Christianity Today* magazine.[1]

> Our lack of biblical literacy has led to a lack of biblical doctrine. LifeWay Research found that while 67 percent of Americans believe heaven is a real place, 45 percent believe there are many ways to get there—including 1 in 5 evangelical Christians. More than half of evangelicals (59 percent) believe the Holy Spirit is a force and not a personal being—in contrast to the orthodox biblical teaching of the Trinity being three Persons in one God. As a whole, Americans, including many Christians, hold

unbiblical views on hell, sin, salvation, Jesus, humanity, and the Bible itself.

The Barna Group did a survey many years ago. At the end of the study, they concluded that the Church at large is biblically illiterate. Some of the results were as follows[2]:

· Less than 50% of those surveyed could name the four gospels.
· 60% of Americans could not name five of the Ten Commandments.
· 82% of Americans believe that "God helps those who help themselves" is a verse in the Bible.
· 12% of adults believed that Joan of Arc was Noah's wife.
· Over 50% of graduating seniors thought Sodom and Gomorrah were husband and wife.
· A considerable number of those surveyed thought the Sermon on the Mount was preached by the late Reverend Billy Graham.

These results reveal the biblical illiteracy that is within America and the Church today. There are those within local churches that have no clue what the Church believes. The Church is more like a club rather than an organization that ascribes to biblical doctrines and values. This needs to change. The beginning of that change starts with basic fundamental foundational doctrines being taught in churches once again.

Repentance from Dead Works

The **first** foundational doctrine that the writer of Hebrews mentions is **repentance from dead works**. Since this is the first foundational doctrine mentioned, I would assume that it is important for us to understand it fully. There is a reason that repentance is the doctrine mentioned first; I believe it is the foundation of all other beliefs. If we don't grasp this one, then all the others will be difficult to understand.

"Repent" in its simplest form means to change. That change is affected in the heart, mind, emotion, and the will of man. A man senses a pricking within his heart that brings forth godly sorrow. His mind is changed as it is renewed with the Word of God. He then makes the choice and decision to walk differently. All these things working together are the manifestation of true heart repentance.

Since we discussed this in detail in an earlier chapter ("*iChange*," chapter 8), I encourage you to review that chapter to refresh or gain greater understanding.

Faith toward God

The **second** foundational doctrine is **faith toward God**. Everything that we receive from God is initiated by faith. The basic process of faith works in this manner. We hear the word of God and choose to believe it. We then confess, declare, and act on that which we have heard and believe. This is active faith.

For us to receive eternal life, faith must be expressed. Faith comes by hearing the Word of God (Romans 10:17). Choosing to believe what we hear and confessing it with our mouths causes faith to be released. This results in the free gift of salvation being received within our lives. The apostle Paul declared that we are saved by grace through faith (Ephesians 2:8). We are not saved through the works of the law, but by faith in the redemptive work that Jesus accomplished through His death, burial, and resurrection.

The Bible declares that with the heart man believes, and with the mouth confession is made unto salvation (Romans 10:10). We see that the faith which begins in our hearts must be expressed through our mouths. There must be an outward expression of that which we believe for faith to be working.

James said that faith without works is dead (James 2:17). He was declaring that true heart faith will be demonstrated in some manner when someone truly believes. Faith is not merely mentally assenting to something that you hear; it requires action and deed to be active, living faith. Faith toward God means that iBelieve and then I act on what I believe.

Doctrine of Baptisms

The **third** foundational doctrine is the **doctrine of baptisms**. The word "baptize" is derived from the Greek word *baptizo* which means to make fully wet, to make overwhelmed, to cover wholly with a fluid, and to wash. There are three different baptisms that we see in the Bible.

To start with, there is the baptism into the body of Christ. First Corinthians 12:13 states, "For by one Spirit we were all baptized into one body." The moment that you are born again, you are baptized into the body of Christ. You are fully saved and instantly made a new creation in Christ Jesus. To be baptized into the body of Christ means that you are fully and wholly covered with the blood of Jesus. At that moment, you no longer have any sin because it has been washed away with His blood.

Baptism into the body of Christ means that iBelong! You have a membership ministry. Every believer has a ministry and function within the church. You were not saved merely to escape hell and go to heaven; you have a purpose. You are not extra baggage in the body of Christ. None of us are an unneeded added appendage. We are not a sixth finger in the Church. You Belong and iBelong!

Water Baptism

The second baptism is baptism in water. Since "baptize" means to make fully wet and to overwhelm, I believe in total submersion. **Water baptism is an outward expression of an inward possession.** It signifies that the old man is dead and buried (when you are submersed in the water), and now we have been raised up with Christ in newness of life (when you come up out of the water). Water baptism makes the declaration that you are alive in Christ (Romans 6:3-5). It is an indication of what transpires in your life through the new birth. We publicly acknowledge our covenant with God through water baptism.

Jesus commanded us to be baptized (Matthew 28:18-20), and He set an example for us by His own baptism. If

Jesus exampled it, then we should do it! On the day of Pentecost, Peter preached that everyone should be baptized (Acts 2:38). Jesus said to baptize in the name of the Father, Son, and Holy Spirit. Peter then exhorted new believers to be baptized in the name of Jesus (the Son).

Someone came to me one day and asked, "How do you baptize people?" My reply was, "In water." They actually were wanting to know if I baptized in Jesus' name or the name of the Father, Son, and Holy Ghost. I personally believe it's better to cover all the bases. So, when we baptize believers, I will say, "In the name of Jesus I baptize you in the name of the Father, Son, and Holy Ghost." All bases covered! Just FYI, Jesus is the Son. We really should not be arguing and debating these types of issues. Instead, we should spend our time baptizing people.

Baptism in the Holy Spirit

The third baptism that we see in the Bible is the baptism in the Holy Spirit. I will share a few brief things concerning this baptism since I've already covered it in the chapter titled "*iFlow*" (Chapter 7).

This baptism is also referred to as the infilling of the Holy Spirit. Jesus said to His disciples that they would receive power after the Holy Spirit came upon them (Acts 1:8). Then, on the day of Pentecost, they were all filled (baptized) with the Holy Spirit and began to speak in tongues as the Spirit gave them utterance.

148

The Baptism in the Holy Spirit is a baptism into the *dunamis* power of God. *Dunamis* is the Greek word translated "power" that means miracle-working power. The baptism in the Holy Spirit is not merely the receiving of a supernatural prayer language, but an infilling of the very power of God through the person of the Holy Spirit. This empowers us for works of service in the kingdom of God.

The first baptism into the body of Christ can be compared to drinking a glass of water. In 1 Corinthians 12, it speaks of baptism into the body of Christ and then says that by one Spirit we have been made to drink. So, salvation is the drink of water, but the infilling of the Holy Spirit is a total submersion and infilling of His power. A drink of water doesn't mean that you are saturated. In the baptism of the Holy Spirit, we are saturated and submersed with the power of the Holy Ghost.

The baptism of the Holy Spirit is evidenced by speaking in tongues. There are five specific instances where believers are baptized in the Holy Spirit. In three of the five, speaking in tongues is specifically mentioned. In the other two, it is inferred. Therefore, speaking in tongues is the initial physical evidence of the baptism in the Holy Spirit.

The baptism in the Holy Spirit is the doorway to the manifestation of the gifts of the Spirit. These gifts are supernatural demonstrations of the power of God that we refer to as the nine manifestation gifts of the Holy Spirit which are mentioned earlier in chapter seven. These gifts are intended to be in operation within the Church today. They are given for the purpose of building, strengthening, and empowering the body of Christ.

Laying On of Hands

The **fourth** foundational doctrine is the laying on of hands. It is a fundamental doctrine and belief of the Church which should be practiced regularly. It was common practice in the early church and should be common practice today. Since this is a foundational doctrine, every believer should be well-versed in their understanding of the purpose for the laying on of hands.

The laying on of hands is exampled in both the Old and New Testaments. Jesus practiced the laying on of hands. He said that believers would lay hands on the sick and they would recover (Mark 16:18). This is one of the signs that is to follow those who believe on the name of the Lord. Therefore, it is something to be practiced by Spirit-filled believers throughout the body of Christ.

The apostle Paul taught and demonstrated the laying on of hands. He exhorted his spiritual son Timothy not to neglect the gift that was given him through the laying on of hands. Ananias, an average believer, laid hands on Paul (Saul) and his sight was restored.

There are three primary purposes for the laying on of hands. First, it is for an impartation of gifts and anointing. Second, it is for the confirmation and recognition of a calling. Thirdly, it is a point of contact for agreement.

Some of the biblical expressions for the laying on of hands is the release of healing, the gifts of the Spirit, the baptism of the Holy Spirit, an impartation of wisdom and grace, prophetic ministry, confirmation and ordination, commissioning and sending, and a point of contact for faith to be released. The laying on of hands is an essential doctrine of the church that should be practiced with frequency within the church today.

All Christians should understand these first four foundational doctrines. They should be active and functioning in the church today. These are truths that we believe and iBelieve! Since iBelieve, iBelong!

1 Ed Stetzer, "The Epidemic of Bible Illiteracy in Our Churches," *Christianity Today Magazine*, July 6, 2015 https://www.christianitytoday.com/edstetzer/2015/july/epidemic-of-bible-illiteracy-in-our-churches.html.

2 "The Scandal of Biblical Illiteracy: It's Our Problem," Dr. R. Albert Mohler, Jr. https://albertmohler.com/2016/01/20/the-scandal-of-biblical-illiteracy-its-our-problem-4/.

C H A P T E R   1 2

iBelieve

PART 2

> BEING ROOTED IN THE FOUNDATIONAL DOCTRINES OF CHRIST WILL PROVIDE THE BASE FROM WHICH GOD CAN ERECT A SPIRITUAL STRUCTURE WITHIN YOUR LIFE THAT WILL STAND THE TEST OF TIME.

For if the dead do not rise, then Christ is not risen. And if Christ is not risen, your faith is futile; you are still in your sins! Then also those who have fallen asleep in Christ have perished. If in this life only we have hope in Christ, we are of all men the most pitiable. But now Christ is risen from the dead, and has become the firstfruits of those who have fallen asleep. For since by man came death, by Man also came the resurrection of the dead (1 Corinthians 15:16-21).

The Resurrection of the Dead

The **fifth** foundational doctrine found in Hebrews 6:1-2 is the resurrection of the dead. The fact that Jesus was raised from the dead is the foundation of our faith. For salvation to be realized, we must believe that God the Father raised Jesus from the dead.

153

Jesus did not have a recreated body; His original physical body was raised from the dead. This is the reason he had scars on His hands when the disciples saw Him after His resurrection. Jesus' body was a resurrected body that enabled him to walk through walls.

Why is this so important? It is because this is what gives us the power to live in victory while on this earth. Paul said if Jesus wasn't resurrected, then our faith is in vain, and we are still in our sins (1 Corinthians 15:17). The understanding of Jesus' physical resurrection empowers us to live victoriously over the flesh and the devil.

This is also the foundation for the understanding that Jesus will come again, the dead in Christ will rise, and those alive will be clothed with immortality.

> For if we believe that Jesus died and rose again, even so God will bring with Him those who sleep in Jesus. For this we say to you by the word of the Lord, that we who are alive and remain until the coming of the Lord will by no means precede those who are asleep. For the Lord Himself will descend from heaven with a shout, with the voice of an archangel, and with the trumpet of God. And the dead in Christ will rise first. Then we who are alive and remain shall be caught up together with them in the clouds to meet the Lord in the air. And thus we shall always be with the Lord. Therefore comfort one another with these words (1 Thessalonians 4:14-18).

A day will come when believers that have died will be united with their resurrected bodies. Exactly how and when these things will happen, I do not know. However, iBelieve! I believe this because this is what God's Word declares.

Salt and Light

The understanding that Jesus will come again should in no way hinder us from doing the will of God and taking dominion in the earth. Some have allowed what has been referred to as the "blessed hope" to become the "blessed dope." They have used the understanding that Jesus will come again as an excuse to disengage from the culture and society. They want to live "in the glory" (the place of spiritual euphoria) while they watch the world travel down the path of destruction. Their thinking is that Jesus will come to rescue us from the wickedness in the world.

However, Jesus said that we are to be salt and light to a perverse generation. As salt, we are called to season (change the taste) and preserve (bring salvation) to the world. As light, we are called to dispel the darkness wherever it may be present. We are not given the luxury of doing nothing. We are called and commissioned to be productive in the kingdom of God. The Father God is glorified when we bear fruit. That means we are to produce.

Resurrection and Translation

When Jesus ascended into heaven, the angel of the Lord told those who were standing there two specific things.

The first was to stop standing around looking up in the air. They needed to get on with the business that Jesus had commissioned them to do. This means that the promise of heaven is not an excuse for us to do nothing in the earth.

The second thing the angel said was that Jesus would in like manner come again. We see a description of this in the above passage of Scripture. It declares what will happen at the time of His appearing. The dead in Christ (believers who have died) will be resurrected, and the believers who remain on the earth will put on immortality and arise to meet the Lord in the air.

I believe there is a reason that the angel of the Lord coupled "this same Jesus will come again" with "why do you stand gazing." We cannot allow the understanding that Jesus is coming to distract us from what needs to be done today. It is important that we are pursuing the purpose and plan of God for our lives rather than sitting on a mountain top waiting for a trumpet to sound.

> Behold, I tell you a mystery: We shall not all sleep, but we shall all be changed—in a moment, in the twinkling of an eye, at the last trumpet. For the trumpet will sound, and the dead will be raised incorruptible, and we shall be changed. For this corruptible must put on incorruption, and this mortal must put on immortality. So when this corruptible has put on incorruption, and this mortal has put on immortality, then shall be brought to pass the saying that is written: "DEATH IS

156

SWALLOWED UP IN VICTORY" (1 Corinthians 15:51-54, emphasis added).

Once again, we see that there will come a day when corruption will put on incorruption and mortality will put on immortality. The dead will be raised, and believers who are living on earth will be changed as they put on immortality. At that moment, the final enemy, Death, will be defeated. Our victory in Christ will literally swallow up death!

There have been many views, ideas, and theories as to exactly how this will take place. We will not take time to discuss them because that is not the purpose of this writing. However, it is vital that we, as Christians, understand that the Lord will come again. Why do we believe that? It is because Jesus said it! Since He said it, iBelieve!

Please hear this: if we can't believe that He will literally come again and that there will be a literal physical resurrection of the dead, then we can't believe John 3:16. Why? It is because the same Jesus said both. The Bible is not a buffet in the sense that you can choose what you want and refuse what you don't want. All of it is meant to be received.

Concerning the time and moment that Jesus will come, we should never speculate. I've been alive long enough to hear many false speculations that didn't come to pass. Many have written books and given dates and times concerning the coming of the Lord. All of them have been wrong so far. Here is some good advice: do the will of God, and let the Father decide when Jesus is to return physically.

The Doctrine of Eternal Judgment (Heaven and Hell)

> And as it is appointed for men to die once, but after this the judgment, so Christ was offered once to bear the sins of many. To those who eagerly wait for Him He will appear a second time, apart from sin, for salvation (Hebrews 9:27-28).

I realize that "judgment" is not a popular word today; however, it is a biblical word. It is a kingdom principle that we must understand and embrace. One of the attributes of our Heavenly Father is justice. He is a God of justice and equity.

If there is no judgment, then there is no right and wrong or sin and righteousness. If there is no penalty for sin, then there was no reason for Jesus to shed His blood and pay the ultimate price. If there is no hell to shun, then sin has no penalty and righteousness has no reward. If there is no heaven to gain, then we are of all men most miserable (that's what Paul said).

Jesus Bore Our Judgment

Concerning judgment for the believer, your sin and my sin was judged on the cross. Jesus took the judgment so that we could go free. His blood settled the debt and salvation was provided for all who believe on Him. We do not need to fear hell or any other type of judgment because Jesus paid the price.

For those who are unsaved, they will receive the judgment for sin because they reject Jesus. Their rejection of His sacrifice will be rewarded with their rejection from heaven and the presence of the Lord. Those who reject the gift of salvation by not believing upon Jesus will ultimately end up in the lake of fire that was originally created for the devil and his angels; it is a place of eternal torment.

Those who receive Jesus' sacrifice and believe upon Him will live forever with Him. They will eternally stand in the presence of the Lord. They will be privileged to rule and reign with Jesus throughout the eons of eternity. Hallelujah!

What You Do Matters

What you do on the earth determines which door you will go through. Every one of us will end up in one of two places: heaven or hell. There is no place in between. Your choice and decision regarding believing and serving Jesus will determine your ultimate destination. This is a choice that only you can make. I encourage you to believe on Jesus, receive His sacrifice, wholly surrender to Him, and live for Him every day of your life. That is the only way to have confidence and surety that you will live with Jesus forever.

> If your hand causes you to sin, cut it off. It is better for you to enter into life maimed, rather than having two hands, to go to hell, into the fire that shall never be quenched— (Mark 9:43).

These are the words of Jesus. He wasn't speaking of an imaginary place called hell. It's important that believers realize that hell is not some make-believe place. Jesus spoke of hell on numerous occasions. Jesus was not merely giving a fairy tale analogy; He spoke of an actual place in existence that is called hell. It is a place that burns eternally. Torment, agony, and pain are all that it offers. Make sure you don't go there—believe on Jesus!

I grew up in church. We heard about heaven and hell on a regular basis. As a little boy, I did not want to go to hell; I wanted to go to heaven. Even though death was a distant thought, heaven and hell were not. I knew that they were real places that existed. At four years old, I committed my life to Jesus, in part, due to the fact that I didn't want to go to hell and wanted to go to heaven.

Most people today only hear the word "hell" being used as an expletive on the job or television. They have never heard hell mentioned from the pulpit. It has been deemed by many church leaders as unpopular, non-relative, and frightening. Unfortunately, because we have failed to articulate principles that embody the doctrine of eternal judgment and talk about hell, many have met their doom.

The Eternal Focus

There is a reason that the foundational doctrine of eternal judgement is specifically mentioned. It is because, without this understanding, people will live without boundaries and in a lawless manner. They will only live for today and the pleasure that it can bring. The understanding of heaven and hell enables us to maintain an eternal focus.

While we should be doing the will of God on the earth now, we should keep focused on the eternal prize at the end. The apostle Paul said that he labored for an eternal crown, not an earthly one (1 Corinthians 9:25). He emphasized that this life on earth was temporary. However, many of us have focused much more on our earthly destiny than our heavenly destination.

I am not saying that we should live our lives in such a manner that we discount our call and purpose on the earth. This book primarily addresses our function within the Church while living here on earth. However, we must always remember that we are not laboring for merely an earthly reward because the heavenly reward is so much greater.

For years, the body of Christ focused solely on heaven and eternity. As revelation and understanding came that we possess a purpose on the earth, many abandoned all teaching and preaching to do with eternal reward and consequence. We must find the correct balance of both truths. Remember that a road has a ditch on both sides. It is not good to fall into either of them.

Eternal Beings that Live Forever

The reality is that we are eternal spirit beings; our spirits will live eternally. How you live your life will determine your address in eternity. Heaven and hell are not a state of mind; they are spiritual geographical locations. Where do you want to live? If you haven't already, make your reservation for heaven now!

161

Once we die, it is not over. We do not go into soul sleep nor do we travel to some sort of spiritual holding tank. Saved people will go to heaven while unsaved people go to hell. There are also rewards that we (the righteous) will receive based upon how we have conducted our lives while living on earth.

> But why do you judge your brother? Or why do you show contempt for your brother? For we shall all stand before the judgment seat of Christ. For it is written: "AS I LIVE, SAYS THE LORD, EVERY KNEE SHALL BOW TO ME, AND EVERY TONGUE SHALL CONFESS TO GOD." So then each of us shall give account of himself to God (Romans 14:10-12, emphasis added).

> Then I saw a great white throne and Him who sat on it, from whose face the earth and the heaven fled away. And there was found no place for them. And I saw the dead, small and great, standing before God, and books were opened. And another book was opened, which is the Book of Life. And the dead were judged according to their works, by the things which were written in the books. The sea gave up the dead who were in it, and Death and Hades delivered up the dead who were in them. And they were judged, each one according to his works. Then Death and Hades were cast into the lake of fire. This is the second death. And anyone not found written in the Book of Life was cast into the lake of fire (Revelation 20:11-15).

Every human being will stand before Almighty God at some point in time. It is there that we all will have to give an account of ourselves. Christians will be judged and rewarded based on their faith in Jesus and their works. Unbelievers will be judged and cast into the lake of fire because their names are not written in the Book of Life. The bottom line is that eternal judgment is something that everyone will face.

There is so much more that could be written on this topic. However, this is a basic understanding of the doctrine of eternal judgment. It is important that we grasp this so that we can live with an eternal perspective. We know that our labor is not in vain in the Lord. Reward will be received both in this life and the one to come.

Judgment is not something that we, as believers, should fear. Jesus took the penalty of hell for me. Therefore, I'm not going there because iBelieve! I will spend eternity with Jesus because iBelieve! You will be with Him too, if you will say, "iBelieve!"

Everything we have talked about within this chapter is foundational in the life of the believer. There are false doctrines and teachings that abound in the hour that we live. The most significant way to combat false teaching is with a solid foundation of God's truth. Being rooted in the foundational doctrines of Christ will provide the base from which God can erect a spiritual structure within your life that will stand the test of time.

These truths will enable you to say, "iBelieve." Not only do iBelieve in Jesus, but iBelieve these biblical doctrines that provide a strong foundation within my life.

CHAPTER 13

iConnect

> **THE GREATEST TOOL THAT ANY OF US POSSESS TO HELP PEOPLE GET CONNECTED TO THE LOCAL CHURCH IS THE LOVE OF GOD.**

Connecting to a church body can be intimidating at times for those who are new members. It is particularly challenging for those who are shy or hurt from past experiences with people. Many times, people are cautious about connecting within a church body because of the fear of the unknown. Therefore, it is important that things be as clearly stated as possible to those who are being introduced to the church and its members.

For many years, until I was in the third grade, I would cry and bury my face in my mother on the first day of school. I was frightened by a new classroom, a new teacher, and faces that I didn't know. The unsureness of the situation caused me to be afraid. I didn't want to connect with anyone. I would finally warm up and find my way to connect in the class. However, it was only because I had no other choice.

Church is an entirely different arena where people can choose to stay or leave. While many people adapt to new situations and surroundings well, some don't. Helping those who are challenged to make connections in a church body is something we all should attempt to do.

I believe that taking an approach that "if God called them to be in our church then they will get connected" is the incorrect attitude to assume. Unfortunately, many people who fail to make a connection within a local church, leave believing that they didn't belong there. The truth is that many of them did belong, but they needed help to make a connection within the church body.

Everyone is Responsible

This is not solely the pastor's responsibility. Nor is this the sole responsibility of the staff. This is the responsibility of everyone in the church. There is no way that one man and his staff can connect with everyone or get them connected. The staff is charged with various duties and will mostly connect with those who are already functioning and working in the church, especially those who function within the areas of their oversight. The responsibility of helping get others connected is something in which the entire church body can assist.

Most people who come to a church arrive there as a direct invitation from someone who is already a member. That member has a greater opportunity to be the bridge of connection for that new individual. They are better positioned to do this than any other person. They already have some form of relationship which gives the new person greater ease in making a connection. The person they already know becomes the bridge for them to get connected.

Think about this: your best friend was a stranger before you met them. Your spouse was an unknown person before you met them. Every person you presently know was an unknown individual at one time. Someone had to "break the ice" for that former stranger to become the close relationship that you now possess.

Let Love Flow

One of the comments that we regularly hear from people who visit our church is about the friendliness of our members and congregants. As the pastor of the church, I have stressed to our leaders and members the importance of reaching out to others. Who knows? The stranger you are looking at today may become your new close friend.

The greatest tool that any of us possess to help people get connected to the local church is the love of God. The reality is people want to be loved. Everybody wants someone to love them; no one wants to be hated and despised. No one wants to feel they are the outcast and merely tolerated.

Paul said that the love of God has been shed abroad in our hearts by the Holy Ghost which means that the love of God resides and dwells within us. It is there waiting to be released. It merely requires us activating it by reaching out beyond our comfort zone and showing interest and concern for someone we may not know.

When we express the love of God, we express the heart of Jesus. When we communicate the love of God, we communicate the essence of His motivation to come to earth and die for our sin. Exhibiting the love of God makes us attractive to others. Everyone is attracted to the display of love and acceptance from others.

When leaders and members of local churches allow God's love to flow, the church will grow. **Love flowing will keep the church growing.** It is imperative that an atmosphere is created that bestows value on everyone who comes through the doors to gather together. It is essential that they know they are needed and appreciated. These are things that some may see as non-spiritual. However, failure to have these things in operation will impede many from the process of getting connected in the church.

We must help new believers get connected. Some will be more assertive and carve out a place for themselves. Others will need to be taken by the hand and guided through the process. We must be willing to do what is necessary to help others in this process of connection.

Take the Plunge

Everything that we learn throughout life requires some aspect of application. No one can learn to swim by staying out of the water while watching Olympic swimming events. We learn to swim by jumping in the water. We must be willing to take the plunge.

Connection in a local church body requires a decision of the heart. It requires that you jump into the middle of everything happening. You can't merely stand on the outside perimeters watching the involvement of others and expect to get connected. You need to jump in with both feet first with no reservations.

I heard Bishop Hamon say for so many years that you learn by doing. He said this in regard to flowing in the gifts of the Spirit. However, this is a principle that governs all aspects of life within the kingdom of God. You will not learn by watching YouTube® videos for the rest of your life. You learn by jumping in the water!

Go ahead and take the plunge. Make a decision to get connected and stay connected. Don't allow the enemy to rob you of the blessing that comes through connection to the church. You will be glad you did.

Final Thoughts

Most of this book has been about belonging and connecting. We have discussed different ways that people can connect within a church body. We have discussed how that every member within the church has a gift and function to fulfill. Those gifts can operate in the church when we are connected to the church.

Although making those connections can be difficult at times, we must still choose to get connected. No one can force another person to get connected within a church body; no law requires it. No leader in the church has the authority to make someone do something they choose not to do. Ultimately, you decide to get connected. In other words, uConnect!

If you are not sure where you fit, then speak with one of the leaders of your church and ask them for guidance. I am sure that they would be thrilled to know you desire to get connected within the church. They will do everything they can to make sure that you find your place of belonging.

After reading this book, I trust you see the importance of getting connected to a local church, an assembly of believers in Jesus. There is a place that God has prepared where you belong. You are not an outcast; you are accepted in the beloved, and you belong.

Don't let another day go by that you believe or feel you are the misfit. Don't let another day go by that you think there is no place for you. You have a destiny and purpose that will be unleashed as you seize the understanding that you belong.

Reflecting back on the dream I shared in the preface of this book, I am now shouting out to you, "We belong to the same tribe." I expect you to do the same thing that the young man in my dream did and run at an accelerated pace. Destiny is waiting to be fulfilled. The purpose of God is calling out to you. It's time to run the race that is set before us.

It is now up to you. Begin taking steps to connect so that you can function within the Church. It must move beyond the words of this book and become the words of your mouth. Begin declaring today: "I am not on the outside because iBelong! I am fearfully and wonderfully made and iBelong! I am a part of the body of Christ and iBelong! God has a place for me to fit in the church today and iBelong!"

ABOUT THE AUTHOR
ROBERT GAY

ROBERT GAY is Senior Pastor and Apostolic founder of High Praise Worship Center in Panama City, Florida. His ministry has a three-fold vision statement: Equipping Believers, Building Families, and Furthering the kingdom of God. Robert provides apostolic oversight to multiple High Praise churches within the United States. He is recognized by many as a prophetic and apostolic voice bringing balance and order into the church today. For complete bio, go to www.highpraisepc.com.

171

172

173

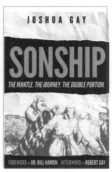

174

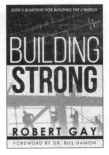

175

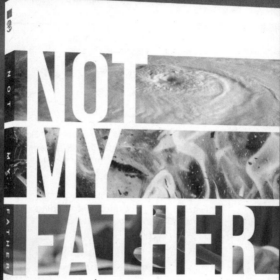

177

HIGHPRAISE
PANAMA CITY

SUN: 10AM // WED: 7PM

CONNECT WITH US ONLINE @HIGHPRAISEPC

HIGHPRAISEPC.COM

pastors
ROBERT & STACEY GAY

SCAN HERE FOR
MORE INFO ABOUT
HIGH PRAISE
PANAMA CITY